A

PROGRAMMER'S

MIND

Dive into Cognitive Patterns
and Mental Models of a
Programmer's Mind

AISHWARYA SHIVA

First Edition 2025

Published by Aishwarya Shiva

INTRODUCTION

In the ever-evolving landscape of technology, the programmer stands as both sculptor and architect, shaping the digital world with an intricate blend of logic and creativity. "A Programmer's Mind" invites you to venture into the cognitive realm where abstract thought transforms into tangible solutions, offering a rare glimpse into the nuanced processes that define a programmer's approach to problem-solving.

At the heart of programming lies the art of translating complex issues into elegant, executable code. This book delves into the mental frameworks and cognitive strategies that programmers employ to dissect problems, devise algorithms, and ultimately craft solutions. It offers readers a window into the mental toolkit that programmers use to navigate the labyrinth of challenges they face daily.

Within these pages, you'll uncover the methodologies that programmers use to decode the seemingly impenetrable. From breaking down problems into manageable components to employing logical reasoning and pattern recognition, the skills explored here are as diverse as they are profound. The narrative illuminates how programmers harness their analytical prowess, creativity, and relentless curiosity to tackle issues ranging from the mundane to the monumental.

"A Programmer's Mind" is not merely a technical manual; it is an exploration of the human intellect at work. It captures the essence of the programmer's journey from confusion to clarity, highlighting the iterative process of trial, error, and refinement that leads to innovation. Beyond the code, it reveals the personal insights and eureka moments that punctuate the programmer's path, offering inspiration to both seasoned developers and aspiring coders alike.

Whether you're a seasoned programmer seeking to refine your craft or a curious novice eager to understand the mental gymnastics behind the code, this book serves as both a guide and a muse. It celebrates the beauty of problem-solving through code and the powerful synergy of logic and imagination that defines the programmer's mind. As you turn the pages, prepare to be captivated by the intricate dance of thought and technology that lies at the heart of programming.

CONTENTS

Chapter 1: The Cognitive Framework

Understanding Cognitive Load

The Brain as a Processor

Analogous to the central processing unit in a computer, the human brain serves as an intricate processor, orchestrating a symphony of neural activities to manage and interpret information. Within its complex architecture lies an unparalleled ability to execute a wide array of cognitive tasks, from basic sensory processing to advanced problem-solving.

The brain's processing power is rooted in its neural networks, which consist of approximately 86 billion neurons, each capable of forming thousands of connections with others. This dense web of connections facilitates the rapid transmission of electrical signals across synapses, enabling the brain to process information at remarkable speeds. Unlike the linear processing of classical computers, the brain operates on a parallel processing model, allowing it to handle multiple tasks simultaneously. This parallelism is what enables humans to perform complex operations such as driving while holding a conversation.

At the core of this processing capability is the brain's ability to learn and adapt. Synaptic plasticity, the process by which synaptic connections strengthen or weaken over time, is fundamental to learning and memory. This dynamic restructuring allows the brain to optimize its processing pathways in response to new experiences, effectively "rewriting" its own code to improve performance. This adaptability is a key distinction between biological processors and their artificial counterparts.

The brain's processing is also distinguished by its use of predictive coding, a model where the brain constantly generates and updates a model of the environment to anticipate sensory inputs. This predictive capability allows for efficient processing by minimizing the cognitive load required to interpret incoming data. The brain essentially functions as a predictive engine, continuously refining its hypotheses about the world to enhance decision-making and perception.

Moreover, the brain exhibits a remarkable level of redundancy and fault tolerance. Unlike a computer processor that may fail due to a single point of failure, the brain can often compensate for damage or loss of function in one area by redistributing tasks to other regions. This resilience is partly due to the plastic nature of neural networks and the brain's modular structure, which allows for localized processing while maintaining global integration.

Despite these impressive capabilities, the brain operates with a level of energy efficiency that far outstrips even the most advanced supercomputers. The human brain consumes about 20 watts of power, a fraction of the energy required by modern computational devices. This efficiency is largely attributed to the sparse coding strategy employed by the brain, where only a small subset of neurons are active at any given time, minimizing energy expenditure while maximizing information processing.

In essence, the brain as a processor is a marvel of evolution, demonstrating a level of complexity and efficiency that continues to inspire advancements in artificial intelligence and computational neuroscience. Its ability to learn, predict, and adapt underpins our understanding of cognition and consciousness, offering a blueprint for developing systems that emulate human intelligence. As we delve deeper into the intricacies of neural processing, we gain insights that not only advance technology but also enhance our understanding of what it means to think and learn.

Mental Models in Programming

Understanding mental models is crucial for programmers as they navigate the complexities of software development. A mental model is an internal representation of external reality, which individuals use to interact with the world around them. In programming, mental models serve as cognitive frameworks that help developers comprehend code, design systems, and troubleshoot errors. These models are vital for effective problem-solving and decision-making, as they enable programmers to conceptualize abstract concepts and translate them into functional code.

Mental models in programming are built through experience and learning. They are shaped by exposure to different programming paradigms, languages, and tools. As developers gain experience, their mental models become more sophisticated, enabling them to predict the behavior of complex systems and anticipate potential issues. A robust mental model allows programmers to abstract details, recognize patterns, and apply solutions from one context to another.

The development of mental models in programming is influenced by several factors. First, the programming language itself plays a significant role. Different languages have unique syntaxes, semantics, and idioms, which shape the way developers think about problems. For instance, object-oriented languages like Java encourage thinking in terms of objects and their interactions, while functional languages like Haskell emphasize immutability and function composition. These paradigms require distinct mental models, and proficiency in multiple languages can enhance a programmer's cognitive flexibility.

Second, the complexity of the task at hand affects the formation of mental models. Simple problems may require straightforward models, while complex systems necessitate layered and intricate representations. Effective programmers can decompose problems into manageable components, creating mental models that mirror the hierarchical structure of the software.

Third, the use of development tools and environments influences mental models. Integrated Development Environments (IDEs), debuggers, and version control systems provide visual cues and feedback, aiding in the construction and refinement of mental models. These tools allow programmers to visualize code execution, track changes, and understand dependencies, enhancing their ability to form accurate mental representations.

The refinement of mental models is an ongoing process. As technologies evolve and new programming paradigms emerge, developers must adapt their mental models to remain effective. Continuous learning through reading, experimentation, and collaboration with peers is essential for keeping mental models up-to-date. Engaging with diverse programming communities and contributing to open-source projects can also expose developers to a variety of perspectives, enriching their cognitive frameworks.

Moreover, cognitive limitations such as working memory constraints and cognitive biases can impact the accuracy and efficiency of mental models. Programmers must be aware of these limitations and employ strategies to mitigate their effects. Techniques such as code refactoring, pair programming, and code reviews can help in refining mental models by providing opportunities for reflection and feedback.

In essence, mental models are indispensable tools for programmers, enabling them to navigate the complexities of software development with agility and precision. By continually refining these models, programmers can enhance their problem-solving skills, adapt to new challenges, and contribute to the advancement of the field. Understanding and leveraging mental models is not merely an intellectual exercise but a practical necessity for any programmer aiming to excel in the dynamic landscape of software development.

Neuroscience and Coding

The human brain, often likened to a highly sophisticated computer, operates through a complex network of neurons, neurotransmitters, and synaptic connections. This intricate system is responsible for processing information, forming memories, and executing complex tasks. Similarly, coding involves the creation of algorithms and programs to perform specific functions. The intersection of neuroscience and coding offers fascinating insights into how programmers can harness their cognitive abilities to enhance coding efficiency and creativity.

The brain's neural networks are comparable to the structures and pathways in computer algorithms. Both systems rely on a series of inputs, processing mechanisms, and outputs to perform tasks. In coding, inputs are data or commands, while in the brain, they are sensory stimuli. The processing involves computation in coding and neural activity in the brain. The outputs are the results of these processes, whether they are program functions or behavioral responses.

Neuroscience reveals that the brain's plasticity, its ability to reorganize itself by forming new neural connections, is a crucial factor in learning and adapting to new coding languages and paradigms. This adaptability is particularly evident in the way programmers can quickly learn and apply new programming languages, leveraging their existing knowledge of syntax and logic to build more complex mental models.

The prefrontal cortex, responsible for executive functions such as problem-solving and decision-making, plays an essential role in coding. It allows programmers to plan, strategize, and troubleshoot effectively, enabling them to break down complex coding problems into manageable components. Additionally, the brain's reward system, primarily mediated by the neurotransmitter dopamine, reinforces learning and motivation, providing the satisfaction that accompanies successful code compilation and execution.

Understanding the cognitive processes involved in coding can lead to improved programming practices. For instance, the concept of cognitive load, which refers to the amount of working memory used during problem-solving, is crucial in coding. Reducing cognitive load by breaking problems into smaller, more manageable tasks can prevent programmer burnout and enhance productivity. Techniques such as pseudocode and flowcharts can assist in visualizing and organizing complex algorithms, thereby reducing cognitive strain.

Moreover, neuroscience emphasizes the importance of rest and mental breaks in maintaining cognitive function. Just as the brain requires periods of rest to consolidate memories and enhance learning, programmers benefit from taking regular breaks to prevent mental fatigue and maintain focus. Techniques such as the Pomodoro Technique, which involves working in short, focused bursts followed by brief breaks, align well with the brain's natural rhythms and can enhance coding efficiency.

In the realm of artificial intelligence, insights from neuroscience have inspired the development of neural networks and machine learning algorithms that mimic the brain's structure and function. These systems, designed to learn and adapt from data, highlight the profound connection between biological and artificial systems. As these technologies evolve, they offer new tools and methods for programmers to explore and integrate into their work.

Ultimately, the interplay between neuroscience and coding underscores the potential for a deeper understanding of both human cognition and computational processes. By leveraging insights from neuroscience, programmers can refine their skills, optimize their workflows, and push the boundaries of what is possible in the digital realm.

Cognitive Bias in Problem Solving

Human cognition, while a powerful tool, is susceptible to various biases that can significantly impact problem-solving abilities in programming. These cognitive biases are systematic patterns of deviation from norm or rationality in judgment, and they often manifest when individuals are processing information and making decisions. Recognizing and understanding these biases is essential for programmers aiming to enhance their problem-solving skills.

One of the most prevalent biases is the **confirmation bias**, which involves favoring information that confirms existing beliefs or hypotheses. In programming, this can lead to overlooking potential errors or alternative solutions. A developer might be so convinced of their initial approach's correctness that they ignore contradictory evidence or fail to thoroughly test other possibilities. To mitigate this, an open-minded review process and seeking peer feedback can be beneficial.

Another common cognitive bias is the **availability heuristic**, where individuals rely on immediate examples that come to mind when evaluating a problem. This can result in overestimating the likelihood of events based on their recent occurrence or prominence in memory. For programmers, this might mean over-relying on solutions that were successful in the past, even if they are not the best fit for the current problem. Encouraging a mindset that values comprehensive research and exploration of new techniques can help counteract this bias.

The **anchoring effect** is another cognitive bias that affects decision-making. It involves relying too heavily on the first piece of information encountered (the "anchor") when making decisions. In a programming context, this might manifest as sticking to the initial requirements or design choices without adequately considering evolving project needs or new insights. Regularly revisiting and revising project assumptions and requirements can help programmers stay adaptable and responsive to change.

The **Dunning-Kruger effect** describes a cognitive bias where individuals with low ability at a task overestimate their ability, while highly competent individuals may underestimate their competence. In programming, this bias can lead to overconfidence in one's solutions, potentially overlooking complex aspects of a problem or dismissing the need for further learning and skill development. Encouraging humility and continuous learning can help programmers maintain a balanced view of their capabilities.

The **overconfidence bias** is closely related, where individuals overestimate their knowledge or abilities. This can be particularly detrimental in collaborative programming environments, where overconfidence can lead to poor decision-making and reduced team input. Fostering a culture of collaboration and valuing diverse perspectives can help mitigate the effects of this bias.

Finally, the **sunk cost fallacy** can trap programmers into continuing down an unproductive path due to the resources already invested, rather than cutting losses and seeking better alternatives. This bias can be countered by developing a strong ability to evaluate projects objectively and making decisions based on current data rather than past investments.

Cognitive biases are an inherent part of human nature, but by becoming aware of these biases and implementing strategies to counteract them, programmers can improve their problem-solving processes. Cultivating an environment that encourages critical thinking, regular feedback, and continuous learning is crucial for minimizing the impact of cognitive biases in programming.

Chapter 2: Problem-Solving Strategies

Algorithmic Thinking

In the realm of programming, the ability to deconstruct complex problems into manageable components is paramount. This skill, often referred to as algorithmic thinking, serves as a cornerstone for effective problem-solving and coding. It involves a systematic approach to identifying the steps required to achieve a particular goal, ensuring that each step is logically sound and contributes to the overall solution.

Algorithmic thinking is not merely a technical skill but a cognitive process that involves a blend of creativity, logic, and precision. It requires programmers to visualize the end result, consider various pathways to reach it, and select the most efficient route. This process is akin to constructing a mental map that guides the programmer through the intricacies of the task at hand.

This mental framework is essential for developing algorithms, which are essentially step-by-step instructions designed to perform specific tasks or solve particular problems. A well-constructed algorithm is both efficient and effective, minimizing the use of resources such as time and computational power, while maximizing output and accuracy.

To cultivate algorithmic thinking, one must engage in a variety of exercises that challenge the mind to think in structured, logical sequences. Puzzles, logical games, and problem-solving tasks are excellent tools for honing this skill. These activities encourage the mind to break down complex scenarios into simpler, more digestible parts, fostering an approach that is both analytical and creative.

In practice, algorithmic thinking involves several key stages. Initially, it requires a clear understanding of the problem. This involves defining the problem space, identifying constraints, and determining the desired outcome. Once the problem is understood, the next step is to devise a plan or strategy. This involves brainstorming possible solutions, evaluating their feasibility, and selecting the one that offers the best balance between complexity and efficiency.

The implementation phase follows, where the chosen algorithm is translated into code. This requires attention to detail and a deep understanding of programming languages and paradigms. During this stage, the programmer must ensure that the code is not only functional but also optimized for performance and readability.

Testing and debugging are integral components of algorithmic thinking. Once the code is written, it must be rigorously tested to ensure it performs as expected under various conditions. Debugging is the process of identifying and rectifying errors, which often involves revisiting the algorithmic plan and making necessary adjustments.

Algorithmic thinking also involves a level of abstraction. Programmers must be able to generalize solutions to apply them to a variety of problems. This requires an understanding of patterns and the ability to create flexible, adaptable algorithms that can be reused in different contexts.

The development of this skill is an ongoing process, requiring continuous practice and refinement. As technology evolves, so too do the challenges faced by programmers. Algorithmic thinking equips them with the tools necessary to navigate this ever-changing landscape, enabling them to devise innovative solutions to increasingly complex problems. It is an essential component of a programmer's toolkit, empowering them to transform abstract ideas into tangible, functional realities.

Debugging the Mind

In the realm of programming, debugging is a critical skill, a systematic process of finding and resolving defects or problems within a computer program. Analogously, the human mind, with its complex neural networks and pathways, occasionally encounters 'bugs'—errors or cognitive distortions that disrupt optimal functioning. Understanding these mental glitches requires a structured approach akin to the methodologies used in software development.

The cognitive architecture of the human brain is intricate, consisting of neurons that communicate through synapses. This biological hardware processes information, formulates thoughts, and dictates behavior. However, just as software can manifest unforeseen errors, the mind can develop cognitive biases, irrational beliefs, or stress-induced distortions. Identifying and addressing these mental inefficiencies is imperative for maintaining psychological well-being and cognitive clarity.

Debugging the mind begins with awareness. Just as a programmer must understand the expected behavior of a program to identify anomalies, individuals must be attuned to their thoughts and emotions. Mindfulness and introspection serve as diagnostic tools, enabling the detection of irregular patterns in thought processes. This self-awareness acts as an initial breakpoint, halting automatic responses to allow for deliberate examination.

The next phase involves the identification of cognitive distortions. These are systematic patterns of deviation from norm or rationality in judgment, often leading to perceptual inaccuracies, illogical interpretations, or emotional upheaval. Common distortions include overgeneralization, catastrophizing, and confirmation bias. By applying techniques akin to code inspection, individuals can scrutinize their thoughts, identifying logical fallacies and emotional triggers.

Subsequently, cognitive restructuring is employed to refactor these distortions. This involves challenging irrational beliefs and replacing them with evidence-based, balanced thoughts. Cognitive Behavioral Therapy (CBT) parallels the iterative process of debugging, where erroneous lines of code are replaced with optimized algorithms. Through this method, individuals can recalibrate their mental frameworks, promoting healthier cognitive functioning.

Crucial to this process is the concept of feedback loops. In programming, feedback loops are used to refine algorithms through continuous testing and adjustment. Similarly, individuals must establish feedback mechanisms that provide insight into the efficacy of their cognitive restructuring efforts. This may involve journaling, engaging in reflective dialogue, or seeking external perspectives to gain objective insights into one's cognitive processes.

Moreover, preventive strategies are essential to minimizing the recurrence of cognitive bugs. Just as programmers employ prophylactic coding practices to avert future errors, individuals can adopt mental hygiene routines. Regular mental exercises, stress management techniques, and cognitive training can fortify mental resilience, decreasing susceptibility to cognitive distortions.

Ultimately, debugging the mind is an ongoing process, a commitment to continual personal development and cognitive optimization. By applying principles from software debugging to the domain of mental health, individuals can enhance their cognitive agility, emotional regulation, and overall psychological resilience. The parallels between debugging code and refining cognition illuminate a path to achieving a more coherent and functional mental state, underscoring the profound interconnectedness of technology and the human mind.

Pattern Recognition

The human brain is an intricate network of neurons that excels at identifying patterns, a skill that has been honed through millennia of evolution. This ability to discern patterns is not just a biological marvel but a crucial component that forms the foundation of programming and computational thinking. In the realm of software development, pattern recognition is the cornerstone that allows programmers to create efficient algorithms, design robust software architectures, and solve complex problems with elegance and precision.

At its core, pattern recognition in programming involves recognizing familiar structures and recurring themes within code and data. This process can be both explicit and implicit. Explicit pattern recognition occurs when developers use established design patterns, such as the Singleton or Observer patterns, to solve common software engineering problems. These patterns provide reusable solutions that streamline the development process, enhance code maintainability, and foster a shared understanding among developers.

Implicit pattern recognition, on the other hand, is akin to intuition and experience. It emerges from prolonged exposure to coding environments and repeated problem-solving. Experienced programmers often "see" the solutions or potential pitfalls in a codebase without deliberate analysis, much like how a seasoned chess player anticipates an opponent's moves. This subconscious recognition is cultivated over time and is a testament to the mind's ability to internalize patterns through continuous practice and reflection.

Machine learning, a subset of artificial intelligence, leverages pattern recognition to enable computers to learn from and make predictions based on data. Algorithms such as neural networks and decision trees are designed to identify patterns within vast datasets, allowing computers to perform tasks ranging from image and speech recognition to natural language processing. In this context, pattern recognition transcends human cognition, enabling machines to process and analyze data at a scale and speed unattainable by humans.

However, the reliance on pattern recognition also presents challenges. The human propensity to identify patterns can lead to cognitive biases, where developers might erroneously identify patterns that do not exist, a phenomenon known as apophenia. This can result in overfitting in machine learning models or misguided assumptions in software design.

To mitigate these challenges, programmers must cultivate a critical mindset, balancing pattern recognition with analytical rigor. This involves questioning assumptions, rigorously testing hypotheses, and employing statistical methods to validate patterns. Additionally, collaboration and peer review are essential practices that can provide diverse perspectives, reducing the risk of cognitive biases and enhancing the robustness of the software.

The art of programming is deeply intertwined with the science of pattern recognition. As technology evolves, the ability to recognize and leverage patterns will remain a vital skill for programmers, enabling them to navigate the complexities of software development with insight and innovation. The continuous interplay between human cognition and computational power will drive the future of programming, as developers harness the strengths of both to create systems that are not only functional but also intelligent and adaptive.

Heuristics in Coding

In the realm of programming, heuristics serve as invaluable tools that guide developers through the intricate maze of code and logic. These are essentially experience-based techniques that facilitate problem-solving, learning, and discovery, without the need for exhaustive search. In the context of coding, heuristics can be understood as practical shortcuts or rules of thumb that programmers employ to make decisions efficiently.

Heuristics in coding are not rigid algorithms but rather flexible strategies that adapt to the dynamic nature of software development. They are derived from empirical evidence and accumulated experience, allowing programmers to navigate the complexities of code with a degree of intuition. This intuitive approach is particularly beneficial in situations where time constraints or incomplete information hinder the application of comprehensive analytical methods.

One common heuristic in coding is the "divide and conquer" strategy. This involves breaking down a complex problem into smaller, more manageable sub-problems. By addressing each sub-problem individually, programmers can simplify the task at hand and incrementally build towards a comprehensive solution. This heuristic not only enhances manageability but also facilitates debugging, as errors can be isolated to specific sections of code.

Another pivotal heuristic is the "rule of simplicity," which advocates for the simplest solution that effectively addresses the problem. This principle is encapsulated in the well-known acronym KISS (Keep It Simple, Stupid). Simplicity in code reduces potential points of failure and enhances readability, making it easier for other developers to understand and maintain the codebase. This heuristic aligns with the minimalist philosophy that pervades much of software engineering, emphasizing clarity and elegance over unnecessary complexity.

The "refactoring" heuristic underscores the importance of continuously improving the structure of existing code without altering its functionality. This iterative process of refinement helps in maintaining code quality over time, ensuring that the codebase remains robust, efficient, and adaptable to future changes. Refactoring embodies the heuristic approach by encouraging developers to be proactive in identifying areas for improvement and acting upon them.

The "use of patterns" heuristic highlights the role of established design patterns in solving recurring problems. By leveraging these patterns, programmers can draw upon proven solutions, thereby increasing efficiency and reducing the likelihood of errors. Design patterns serve as templates that encapsulate best practices, enabling developers to implement solutions that are both effective and scalable.

Heuristics also extend to debugging, where strategies such as "binary search debugging" can expedite the identification of errors. This involves systematically narrowing down the location of a bug by dividing the code into sections and testing each section iteratively. Such heuristics streamline the debugging process, allowing developers to pinpoint and resolve issues more swiftly.

In conclusion, heuristics are indispensable in the programmer's toolkit, providing a framework for decision-making in the face of complexity and uncertainty. By embracing these heuristics, developers can enhance their problem-solving capabilities, improve code quality, and ultimately contribute to the creation of more reliable and efficient software systems. The utilization of heuristics exemplifies the confluence of art and science in programming, where intuition and logic coexist to drive innovation and progress.

Iterative Approaches

In the realm of programming, iterative approaches stand as a cornerstone for problem-solving and application development. Iteration, by its nature, involves repeating a set of instructions until a specific condition is met, allowing for the refinement and enhancement of solutions through successive approximations. This method is not only an essential aspect of algorithmic design but also reflects a cognitive process inherent in the programmer's mindset.

At the core of iterative approaches lies the concept of loops, which enable programmers to execute a block of code multiple times. The most common types of loops include for-loops, while-loops, and do-while loops, each offering a distinct mechanism for iteration. For-loops, for instance, are particularly useful when the number of iterations is known beforehand, providing a precise control structure for executing code a specific number of times. Conversely, while-loops and do-while loops are more suited for situations where the iteration count is determined dynamically, based on runtime conditions.

Beyond these basic constructs, iterative approaches are also exemplified in more sophisticated algorithmic paradigms such as recursion. Recursion, although often perceived as a separate concept, is inherently iterative as it involves a function calling itself with modified arguments until a base condition is satisfied. This recursive iteration is especially powerful in problems that can be broken down into smaller sub-problems, such as those encountered in divide-and-conquer algorithms.

The iterative process is not limited to mere execution of instructions; it encompasses a broader strategy of incremental development and testing. In software engineering, iterative development models, such as Agile and Scrum, emphasize the importance of developing software in small, manageable increments. This approach allows for continuous feedback and adaptation, ensuring that the final product evolves in alignment with user needs and technological advancements. Each iteration serves as a learning cycle, where insights gained from testing and user feedback inform subsequent iterations, leading to a progressively refined product.

Moreover, iterative approaches foster a mindset of flexibility and adaptability within programmers. The practice of repeatedly refining code encourages a deeper understanding of the problem space and fosters creativity in devising solutions. It also necessitates a rigorous approach to debugging and optimization, as each iteration provides an opportunity to identify inefficiencies and improve performance.

In algorithmic problem-solving, iterative methods are often preferred over their direct counterparts due to their simplicity and ease of implementation. For example, iterative solutions to problems such as those involving searching and sorting are typically more intuitive and less prone to errors than recursive solutions, which can be complex and challenging to optimize.

Ultimately, the iterative approach is emblematic of the programmer's mindset, grounded in the principles of continuous improvement and adaptability. It underscores the dynamic nature of programming, where solutions are not static but evolve through a process of experimentation and refinement. By embracing iterative methodologies, programmers not only enhance their technical proficiency but also cultivate a mindset attuned to the ever-changing landscape of technology and user expectations. Thus, iteration is not merely a technique but a fundamental aspect of the intellectual framework that defines a programmer's approach to problem-solving.

Chapter 3: The Architecture of Thought

Modular Thinking

A programmer's mind is an intricate web of logic, creativity, and problem-solving prowess. At its core is the ability to deconstruct complex problems into manageable components. This approach, often referred to as modular thinking, is an essential cognitive strategy that underpins efficient programming practices.

Modular thinking enables programmers to break down a system into discrete, independent modules or units, each responsible for a specific function. This methodology is akin to the divide-and-conquer strategy, where a problem is segmented into smaller, more manageable parts that can be tackled individually. Through this approach, programmers can isolate errors, enhance code readability, and streamline the debugging process.

The concept of modularity is not new. It has long been a foundational principle in various fields, from mathematics to engineering. In programming, however, it has evolved to become a central tenet, guiding the development of software architectures and influencing the design of programming languages. The implementation of modular thinking is evident in practices such as object-oriented programming, where classes and objects encapsulate data and behavior, promoting reusability and scalability.

One of the fundamental advantages of modular thinking is its facilitation of code reuse. By designing modules that perform specific functions, programmers can create libraries of reusable code that can be employed across multiple projects. This not only accelerates development but also ensures consistency and reliability in software applications. Reusable code modules can be thought of as building blocks that, when combined, form a cohesive system. These blocks can be modified or replaced without affecting the overall system, thus enhancing flexibility and adaptability.

Moreover, modular thinking aids in improving collaboration among development teams. In large-scale projects, where numerous programmers work concurrently, modularity allows for parallel development. Different team members can work on separate modules simultaneously, minimizing dependencies and reducing the likelihood of conflicts. This collaborative aspect is further reinforced by the use of version control systems, which track changes and manage contributions from multiple developers.

The cognitive processes involved in modular thinking are deeply aligned with the nature of human problem-solving. The human brain naturally seeks patterns and structures, making it adept at compartmentalizing information. This cognitive tendency is mirrored in programming, where abstraction and decomposition are key strategies for managing complexity. By leveraging these inherent capabilities, programmers can create systems that are not only functional but also elegant in their simplicity.

In practice, the application of modular thinking requires discipline and foresight. It necessitates a thorough understanding of the problem domain and a meticulous approach to designing interfaces and interactions between modules. This involves defining clear boundaries and establishing protocols for communication between components, ensuring that each module performs its function efficiently while integrating seamlessly with others.

In essence, modular thinking is a cognitive framework that empowers programmers to navigate the complexities of software development. It is a testament to the synergy between human cognition and technological innovation, underscoring the programmer's role as both an architect and a craftsman in the digital age. By embracing modularity, programmers can harness the full potential of their cognitive abilities, transforming abstract ideas into tangible, functional systems.

Abstraction Layers

In the realm of computing, abstraction serves as a pivotal concept that enables programmers to manage complexity by simplifying intricate systems into more comprehensible entities. Abstraction layers are integral to this process, serving as the scaffolding upon which software architectures are built. Each layer abstracts specific details, providing a structured pathway from the high-level application logic down to the low-level hardware interactions.

At its core, an abstraction layer is a mechanism that hides the complex details of a system, presenting a simplified interface to the user or the layer above it. This separation of concerns allows programmers to focus on the task at hand without being overwhelmed by the intricacies of underlying components. By organizing systems into hierarchical layers, each responsible for a particular aspect of the program, abstraction facilitates modular design and enhances code maintainability and scalability.

Consider the common architecture of a computer system, which typically comprises multiple layers of abstraction. At the highest level, application software interacts with users, providing an interface to perform specific tasks. This layer abstracts the details of underlying operations, presenting them in a user-friendly manner. Below this, the operating system layer manages resources, such as memory and processing power, and provides essential services to applications. It abstracts hardware complexities, offering a consistent interface for software developers.

Further down, we encounter the hardware abstraction layer, which serves as a bridge between the operating system and the physical components of the computer. This layer abstracts hardware specifics, enabling the operating system to function across different hardware platforms without requiring modification. By isolating hardware dependencies, abstraction layers promote portability and flexibility in software development.

In programming languages, abstraction is realized through constructs such as functions, classes, and data types. Object-oriented programming, in particular, leverages abstraction to encapsulate data and behavior within objects, allowing for the creation of reusable and modular code. This encapsulation hides the internal state of objects, exposing only the necessary interfaces for interaction, thus reducing complexity and enhancing code clarity.

The benefits of abstraction layers extend beyond code organization. They also play a crucial role in error handling and debugging. By compartmentalizing functionality, abstraction layers localize potential points of failure, making it easier to identify and rectify issues. This modularity not only simplifies maintenance but also facilitates collaborative development, as teams can work on different layers independently without interfering with each other's progress.

However, abstraction is not without its trade-offs. Excessive abstraction can lead to performance overhead, as each layer introduces additional processing. This necessitates a careful balance between abstraction and efficiency, ensuring that the system remains performant while retaining its modularity. Nevertheless, the advantages of abstraction layers in managing complexity, enhancing code readability, and supporting system evolution far outweigh the potential downsides.

In essence, abstraction layers are indispensable tools in the programmer's arsenal, providing a structured framework to navigate the complexities of modern computing systems. By abstracting away unnecessary details, they empower developers to craft sophisticated software solutions that are robust, scalable, and adaptable to the ever-evolving technological landscape. As computing systems continue to grow in complexity, the strategic use of abstraction layers will remain a fundamental principle in software engineering, shaping the way programmers conceptualize and build the technological world.

Hierarchical Structuring

In the realm of programming, the ability to think hierarchically is not merely a skill but a necessity. This cognitive approach allows programmers to manage complexity by dividing tasks into manageable components. Hierarchical structuring is deeply rooted in the fundamental principles of computer science, echoing the architecture of both data structures and algorithms.

At its core, hierarchical structuring in programming draws parallels with the tree-like structures prevalent in nature and technology. These structures facilitate efficient information retrieval and processing, akin to how a tree's branches allow for nutrient distribution in a plant. Programmers often employ hierarchical models to break down large problems into smaller, more tractable sub-problems. This decomposition is crucial as it aligns with the divide-and-conquer paradigm, enabling the development of scalable and maintainable code.

Furthermore, hierarchical thinking is instrumental in object-oriented programming (OOP), where class inheritance creates a multi-level hierarchy. This allows for the abstraction of common characteristics into base classes, thereby promoting code reuse and reducing redundancy. By leveraging inheritance, programmers can build complex systems with a clear and organized structure, enabling easier debugging and enhancement of code functionalities.

In addition to OOP, hierarchical structuring is evident in data management, particularly in database design. Relational databases utilize hierarchical models to organize data into tables connected through primary and foreign keys. This structure not only ensures data integrity but also optimizes query performance. Similarly, hierarchical data formats such as XML and JSON are used extensively in data interchange, offering a clear structure that mirrors the nested nature of data, allowing for straightforward parsing and manipulation.

The hierarchical nature of software development projects is another facet where this structuring approach manifests itself. Projects are often broken down into modules, each responsible for a specific functionality. This modular approach facilitates parallel development, where different teams can work on separate modules simultaneously, thereby accelerating the development process. Additionally, it aids in the identification of dependencies and potential bottlenecks, allowing for more effective project management.

Moreover, hierarchical structuring is pivotal in algorithm design, particularly in search and sort operations. Algorithms such as binary search and quicksort utilize hierarchical strategies to achieve optimal performance. For instance, binary search divides the dataset into two halves, recursively narrowing down the search space, thereby achieving logarithmic time complexity. Similarly, quicksort employs a recursive partitioning strategy, effectively sorting data through hierarchical division.

The human brain itself functions hierarchically, processing information in layers of abstraction, which aligns with how programmers approach problem-solving. This cognitive synergy underscores the importance of hierarchical structuring in programming, as it mirrors natural human thought processes, thereby enhancing comprehension and innovation.

In essence, hierarchical structuring is a cornerstone of programming that underpins various paradigms and practices. By organizing code, data, and projects into hierarchical models, programmers can manage complexity, improve efficiency, and foster a deeper understanding of the systems they create. As technology continues to evolve, the principles of hierarchical structuring will remain integral to the advancement of software development, serving as a testament to the enduring power of organized thought in the digital age.

Parallel Processing

In the realm of modern computing, the ability to execute multiple instructions simultaneously is not just advantageous but essential. This capability, known as parallel processing, has revolutionized the way programmers approach problem-solving, enabling the efficient handling of complex computational tasks. As processors have evolved, from single-core to multi-core architectures, the paradigm of parallel processing has become increasingly relevant to both hardware and software development.

The core premise of parallel processing lies in its ability to divide a task into smaller sub-tasks that can be processed concurrently. This is achieved through a variety of techniques, including data parallelism, task parallelism, and pipeline parallelism. Each of these methodologies leverages the inherent architecture of multi-core processors to enhance computational efficiency and reduce execution time.

Data parallelism involves distributing subsets of data across multiple processing units, allowing each unit to perform the same operation on different pieces of data simultaneously. This approach is particularly effective in operations that involve large datasets, such as matrix multiplication or image processing. Task parallelism, on the other hand, focuses on executing different tasks concurrently, which may or may not require communication between them. This form of parallelism is beneficial in scenarios where tasks are independent, such as running multiple applications simultaneously.

Pipeline parallelism, inspired by the assembly line concept, involves dividing a task into a series of stages, with each stage being processed concurrently. This technique is particularly useful in scenarios where tasks need to be processed in a specific sequence, such as in video encoding or decoding.

The implementation of parallel processing is not without its challenges. Synchronization, communication overhead, and load balancing are critical factors that influence the efficiency of parallel systems. Synchronization ensures that multiple threads or processes access shared resources without conflict, while communication overhead refers to the time and resources required to coordinate tasks across different processing units. Load balancing aims to distribute tasks evenly across processors to prevent some units from being overburdened while others remain idle.

To address these challenges, programmers employ a variety of tools and frameworks designed to facilitate parallel computing. OpenMP, MPI (Message Passing Interface), and CUDA are among the most prevalent, each catering to different aspects of parallelism. OpenMP simplifies the process of parallelizing code in shared-memory architectures, while MPI is ideal for distributed-memory systems. CUDA, developed by NVIDIA, harnesses the power of GPUs to execute thousands of threads concurrently, making it particularly effective for data-intensive operations.

Parallel processing has profound implications for the development of artificial intelligence, machine learning, and big data analytics. These fields demand the processing of vast amounts of data in real-time, a feat made feasible by the concurrent execution capabilities of modern processors. As technology continues to evolve, the principles of parallel processing will remain a cornerstone of computational progress, driving innovation and expanding the horizons of what is achievable through programming.

Understanding the intricacies of parallel processing equips programmers with the tools to optimize performance and scalability in their applications. It challenges traditional sequential thinking, encouraging a mindset that embraces concurrency and collaboration between computing units. As we continue to push the boundaries of computational capabilities, the principles of parallel processing will undoubtedly play a pivotal role in shaping the future of programming and technology.

Sequential Logic

The landscape of computational theory and practice is intricately woven with the threads of logic, and among these, sequential logic stands as a cornerstone. It represents a paradigm wherein the output is not solely determined by the current inputs but also by the history of past inputs. This temporal dimension introduces a complexity that is pivotal in the design and functioning of digital circuits, thereby influencing the programmer's cognitive framework.

In sequential logic, a fundamental distinction is drawn from its combinational counterpart. While combinational logic is characterized by outputs that are direct functions of present inputs, sequential logic incorporates memory elements, allowing the system to possess a state. This stateful nature enables the execution of tasks that require a sequence of operations, thus reflecting the dynamic nature of real-world processes.

Memory elements such as flip-flops and latches serve as the building blocks of sequential logic. Flip-flops, in particular, are bistable devices capable of storing a binary digit, or bit. They are synchronized by a clock signal, which dictates when the state of the flip-flop is to be updated. This synchronization is crucial, as it ensures that state changes occur in a predictable manner, thus maintaining the integrity of the system's operation.

The clock signal itself is a periodic waveform that orchestrates the timing of state transitions in a sequential circuit. It is the heartbeat of the system, providing a rhythm that aligns the operations of various components. The frequency of the clock determines the speed at which the system can process information, influencing the overall performance of the digital circuit.

Sequential circuits are broadly categorized into two types: synchronous and asynchronous. Synchronous sequential circuits rely on the clock signal for state transitions, ensuring that all parts of the circuit update simultaneously. This uniformity simplifies the design and analysis of the circuit, making it the preferred choice in many applications.

Conversely, asynchronous sequential circuits do not depend on a global clock, allowing state changes to occur in response to input changes. While this can lead to faster response times in certain scenarios, it introduces complexities in ensuring stable and predictable behavior, as the absence of a clock can result in race conditions and hazards.

The implications of sequential logic extend beyond hardware design into the realm of software development. Programmers must cultivate an understanding of stateful systems, as many software applications exhibit behaviors analogous to sequential circuits. For instance, a state machine model is often employed in software to manage complex control flow, mirroring the operation of a sequential circuit.

Understanding sequential logic equips programmers with the tools to design systems that effectively manage state and sequence operations, whether in hardware or software. It fosters a mindset attuned to temporal considerations, enabling the creation of robust, efficient systems that can navigate the intricacies of real-world applications. As such, sequential logic not only enriches the programmer's technical repertoire but also enhances their capacity to conceptualize and implement solutions that are both innovative and grounded in fundamental principles.

Chapter 4: Language and Logic

Syntax and Semantics

Flow Control

In the realm of programming, the concept of flow control serves as the very backbone of computational logic, dictating the sequence and conditions under which specific blocks of code are executed. An adept understanding of flow control mechanisms is indispensable for a programmer seeking to craft efficient, reliable, and robust software solutions.

At the heart of flow control lies the conditional statement, a fundamental construct that allows a program to make decisions. The most basic form of this is the 'if' statement, which evaluates a condition: if true, a block of code is executed; if false, the program may proceed to an 'else' block or skip execution entirely. This binary decision-making process is akin to a fork in the road, where the path chosen depends on the truth value of a given condition.

The efficacy of conditional statements is amplified when combined with logical operators such as 'and', 'or', and 'not', allowing for more complex conditional expressions. These operators enable programmers to combine multiple conditions into a single statement, thus enhancing the flexibility and power of decision-making capabilities within a program.

Beyond conditional statements, flow control encompasses iterative constructs, commonly referred to as loops. Loops, such as 'for', 'while', and 'do-while', facilitate the repeated execution of a block of code, either a predetermined number of times or until a specified condition is met. This iterative process is crucial for tasks that require repetitive actions, such as processing elements in a collection or performing operations until convergence is achieved.

The 'for' loop is particularly useful when the number of iterations is known beforehand. It provides a concise syntax for initializing a counter, setting a termination condition, and incrementing the counter in each iteration. Conversely, the 'while' loop is preferred when the number of iterations is not predetermined, continuing execution as long as its condition remains true.

In certain scenarios, a 'do-while' loop may be employed, ensuring that the loop's body is executed at least once before the condition is evaluated. This guarantees that the loop's code block is entered, an essential feature when the initial execution is required regardless of conditions.

Flow control constructs also include the 'switch' statement, a multi-way branch that provides an elegant solution for decision-making scenarios involving multiple discrete values. Unlike a series of 'if-else' statements, a 'switch' statement evaluates a single expression and executes the corresponding code block for the matching value, enhancing readability and maintainability.

Exception handling represents a sophisticated form of flow control, designed to manage errors and exceptional conditions that arise during program execution. The 'try', 'catch', and 'finally' blocks form the cornerstone of exception handling, allowing a program to gracefully recover from errors without abrupt termination. By encapsulating code that may throw exceptions within a 'try' block and providing corresponding 'catch' blocks to handle specific exceptions, programmers ensure that their software can handle unexpected situations with resilience.

In essence, flow control is a testament to the structured nature of programming, providing the necessary tools to dictate the precise order of operations and ensure that programs respond appropriately to varying conditions and inputs. Mastery of these constructs is essential for any programmer endeavoring to harness the full potential of computational logic.

Logical Operators

In the realm of programming, logical operators serve as pivotal tools in decision-making processes, enabling the creation of intricate conditions and flow control within algorithms. These operators, fundamental to boolean algebra, facilitate the evaluation and manipulation of truth values, which are integral to the operations of conditional statements, loops, and complex data structures.

Logical operators are chiefly categorized into three types: AND, OR, and NOT. Each operator plays a distinct role in constructing logical expressions, which can be evaluated to either true or false, thus determining the execution path of a program.

The AND operator, denoted typically by `andand` in many programming languages, is employed to combine two or more expressions. The resultant expression yields true only if all constituent expressions are true. This operator is instrumental in scenarios where multiple conditions must be simultaneously satisfied. For instance, in user authentication systems, a valid username AND a correct password must be provided for access to be granted.

Conversely, the OR operator, represented as `||`, allows for flexibility by evaluating to true if at least one of its component expressions is true. This operator is particularly useful when multiple pathways can lead to a satisfactory outcome. For example, a program might proceed if a user has either administrative privileges OR special access rights. The NOT operator, denoted by `!`, is a unary operator that inverts the truth value of its operand. It is essential for scenarios where the negation of a condition is required. In essence, if a certain condition evaluates to true, applying the NOT operator will render it false, and vice versa. This operator is often used to ensure a condition is not met before proceeding with a specific task, such as checking if a file does NOT exist before creating it.

Combining these operators allows for the construction of complex logical expressions that can model sophisticated decision-making processes. The precedence and associativity rules govern the order of evaluation for these operators, ensuring that expressions are parsed correctly. Parentheses are often utilized to explicitly define evaluation order, enhancing readability and preventing logical errors.

In addition to their use in control flow, logical operators are instrumental in data filtering, search algorithms, and validation checks. They enable programmers to define precise criteria for selecting data from large datasets, ensuring that only relevant information is processed.

Understanding and effectively utilizing logical operators are crucial skills for programmers, as they directly impact the robustness and efficiency of algorithms. Mastery of these operators enhances a programmer's ability to design and implement solutions that are both logical and efficient, reflecting the core principles of computational thinking.

Ultimately, logical operators are indispensable in translating human reasoning into a form that computers can execute, bridging the gap between abstract concepts and executable instructions. Their role in programming underscores the importance of logic in software development, providing the foundation upon which complex systems are built and maintained. Through the adept application of logical operators, programmers can ensure their code not only meets functional requirements but also adheres to high standards of clarity and performance.

Error Handling

In the realm of programming, error handling emerges as a pivotal component, encapsulating the strategies and methodologies employed to manage and resolve anomalies that arise during code execution. Errors, often perceived as inevitable disruptions, demand a systematic approach to ensure the robustness and reliability of software systems. This subchapter delves into the intricacies of error handling, elucidating its significance and exploring various paradigms and techniques that constitute this domain.

The fundamental premise of error handling is the anticipation of potential faults and the implementation of mechanisms to address them effectively. These faults may manifest as syntax errors, runtime exceptions, or logical discrepancies, each necessitating a distinct response strategy. The primary objective is to ensure that the program can gracefully recover from unforeseen conditions, thereby maintaining its intended functionality and enhancing user experience.

A comprehensive error handling strategy begins with the identification and classification of errors. Syntax errors, often detected during the compilation phase, are relatively straightforward to rectify as they typically involve violations of language rules. Runtime errors, however, pose a greater challenge, as they occur during execution and may arise from unpredictable inputs or resource constraints. Logical errors, on the other hand, stem from flawed algorithms or misinterpretations of problem requirements, necessitating a thorough review of the code logic.

One prevalent approach to runtime error handling involves the use of try-catch blocks, a construct that allows programmers to anticipate and manage exceptions. By encapsulating potentially erroneous code within a try block, and specifying catch clauses to handle specific exceptions, developers can ensure that the program remains operational even when errors occur. This technique not only aids in isolating problematic segments but also facilitates the implementation of corrective actions, such as resource deallocation or user notification.

Error handling is further augmented by the incorporation of logging mechanisms, which serve as diagnostic tools to record error occurrences and trace their origins. By maintaining detailed logs, developers can conduct post-mortem analyses to identify recurring issues and refine their codebase accordingly. Additionally, logging provides invaluable insights during the debugging process, enabling a more targeted and efficient resolution of complex errors.

Another critical aspect of error handling is the principle of fail-safe defaults, which advocates for the adoption of conservative fallback behaviors in the event of failure. This principle underscores the importance of designing systems that prioritize safety and stability over aggressive performance optimizations. By ensuring that default states do not compromise the integrity of the system, developers can mitigate the impact of errors and safeguard critical operations.

In parallel, the practice of writing defensive code further strengthens error handling capabilities. This involves the proactive validation of inputs, assumptions, and invariants, thereby preempting potential errors before they manifest. Defensive programming encourages a mindset of vigilance and foresight, recognizing that errors are not merely bugs to be squashed, but opportunities for learning and improvement.

In sum, error handling is an indispensable facet of programming, demanding a balance between proactive prevention and reactive resolution. Through a combination of structured exception management, comprehensive logging, and defensive coding practices, developers can cultivate resilient software systems that withstand the uncertainties of execution. This holistic approach not only enhances the reliability of applications but also fosters a deeper understanding of the underlying complexities inherent in the programming landscape.

Functional Paradigms

The functional programming paradigm offers a distinct approach to software development, characterized by its emphasis on immutability, first-class functions, and declarative style. Unlike imperative paradigms that focus on describing how a program operates, functional programming centers on what the program should accomplish, leveraging mathematical functions as the primary building blocks.

At the core of functional programming lies the concept of pure functions. These functions are deterministic, meaning that for any given set of inputs, they produce the same output without causing side effects. This property ensures predictability and reliability, which are crucial for constructing robust software systems. Pure functions also facilitate reasoning about code, as they can be composed to build more complex operations without unintended interactions.

Another fundamental aspect is immutability, which dictates that data should not be modified after its creation. Instead of altering existing data structures, functional programs produce new ones, preserving the original data. This approach reduces the risk of unintended changes and enhances concurrency, as immutable data can be safely shared across multiple threads without synchronization issues.

Higher-order functions, which can accept other functions as arguments or return them as results, are pivotal in functional programming. They enable the creation of abstract and reusable code patterns, fostering modularity and reducing redundancy. Commonly used higher-order functions include map, filter, and reduce, which offer elegant solutions for transforming and aggregating data structures.

Closely related to higher-order functions is the concept of function composition, where simple functions are combined to form more complex ones. This promotes code reusability and clarity, allowing developers to construct intricate operations by chaining simpler functions together. The result is code that is not only concise but also easier to understand and maintain.

Functional programming also embraces lazy evaluation, a technique where expressions are not evaluated until their values are needed. This can lead to performance improvements by avoiding unnecessary computations and enabling the handling of infinite data structures. Lazy evaluation is often implemented through constructs such as streams, which allow for efficient and deferred computation.

Pattern matching, another hallmark of functional paradigms, provides a mechanism for deconstructing data structures and branching logic based on their shape. This feature simplifies the handling of complex data types and enhances code readability by clearly delineating different cases and their corresponding actions.

Languages that support functional programming, such as Haskell, Scala, and Clojure, often provide robust type systems that further enhance program correctness. These type systems can enforce constraints at compile time, catching potential errors early in the development process and reducing runtime failures.

Despite its advantages, functional programming is not without challenges. Its abstraction level can pose a steep learning curve for developers accustomed to imperative paradigms. Additionally, certain tasks, such as I/O operations, may require specific handling to maintain purity. Nonetheless, the growing interest in functional programming reflects a broader recognition of its potential to produce reliable, maintainable, and scalable software solutions in the modern computing landscape.

Chapter 5: The Emotional Algorithm

Emotional Intelligence in Coding

The realm of coding, often perceived as a domain dominated by logic and technical acumen, is increasingly recognizing the significance of integrating emotional intelligence (EI) into its frameworks. This integration is not merely an adjunct to technical skill but a crucial component that enhances problem-solving abilities, fosters collaborative environments, and leads to more innovative solutions.

Emotional intelligence, broadly defined as the capacity to recognize, understand, and manage one's own emotions while recognizing, understanding, and influencing the emotions of others, plays a pivotal role in the field of programming. As programmers navigate complex systems, they must also navigate the complexities of human interaction, both within their teams and in understanding the needs and expectations of end-users.

In coding practices, the ability to manage one's emotions is paramount. The iterative nature of coding, characterized by cycles of debugging and testing, often leads to frustration and stress. A programmer with high emotional intelligence can maintain composure, employ resilience, and manage stress effectively, thus maintaining productivity and creativity even under pressure. This emotional regulation is crucial in sustaining long-term engagement with projects and preventing burnout.

Moreover, emotional intelligence enhances team dynamics. Coding projects are rarely solitary endeavors; they require collaboration and communication. Programmers with high EI are skilled in empathy, allowing them to understand and respect diverse perspectives within a team. This empathetic approach fosters a supportive environment where team members feel valued, leading to increased morale and productivity. Furthermore, effective communication, a component of emotional intelligence, ensures that ideas and feedback are exchanged clearly and constructively, minimizing conflicts and misunderstandings.

In the context of coding, emotional intelligence also intersects with creativity. Creativity in programming is not solely about writing innovative code but also about conceptualizing novel solutions to complex problems. Emotional intelligence equips programmers with the ability to embrace uncertainty and ambiguity, key conditions under which creativity flourishes. By being attuned to their own emotional states and those of others, programmers can create an environment conducive to open-minded exploration and risk-taking, essential elements in the creative process.

The impact of emotional intelligence extends beyond individual and team productivity to the end-user experience. A programmer with high EI is more adept at understanding user needs and anticipating potential usability issues, leading to more intuitive and user-friendly software solutions. By considering the emotional responses of users, programmers can design interfaces that not only meet functional requirements but also provide a positive emotional experience, thereby enhancing user satisfaction and engagement.

In summary, the integration of emotional intelligence into the domain of coding is not supplementary but essential. It serves as a bridge between the technical and human aspects of programming, fostering environments where innovation thrives, teams collaborate effectively, and solutions are crafted with both logic and empathy. As the field continues to evolve, the role of emotional intelligence in shaping the future of coding will only become more pronounced, underscoring its importance as a fundamental skill for programmers in the modern age.

Stress and Performance

In the field of programming, the relationship between stress and performance is a subject of considerable interest, given the intense cognitive demands faced by programmers. Stress, defined as the body's response to any demand or challenge, can have both deleterious and beneficial effects on performance, contingent upon its intensity and duration.

At an optimal level, stress can enhance cognitive function by triggering the release of adrenaline, which sharpens focus and increases alertness. This state, often referred to as "eustress," can lead programmers to achieve heightened productivity and creativity, facilitating problem-solving and innovative thinking. The stimulation provided by eustress can drive programmers to meet deadlines effectively and tackle complex coding challenges with enhanced vigor.

However, when stress exceeds an individual's threshold, it transitions into "distress," which can impede cognitive function. Distress can lead to a cascade of physiological and psychological responses that detract from a programmer's ability to concentrate and process information effectively. Chronic exposure to high stress levels can result in burnout, characterized by mental fatigue, decreased motivation, and a decline in cognitive performance.

The impact of stress on a programmer's performance is mediated by several factors, including individual differences in stress tolerance, coping mechanisms, and the nature of the task at hand. For instance, programmers with high resilience may exhibit superior performance under stress due to adaptive coping strategies that mitigate the negative effects of stress. Conversely, those with low resilience might experience significant performance decrements under similar conditions.

The complexity and novelty of a programming task also influence how stress affects performance. Routine tasks may allow for better stress management as they engage procedural memory and require less cognitive effort. In contrast, novel tasks that demand higher-order cognitive processes, such as working memory and problem-solving, may exacerbate the detrimental effects of stress on performance.

Moreover, the work environment plays a pivotal role in modulating stress levels and performance. A supportive work culture that encourages collaboration and provides resources for stress management can buffer the negative impact of stress. Conversely, environments characterized by high workload, lack of autonomy, and poor communication can exacerbate stress and hinder performance.

Interventions to manage stress and optimize performance in programming contexts focus on both individual and organizational strategies. On an individual level, techniques such as mindfulness meditation, time management, and cognitive-behavioral strategies can enhance stress resilience and cognitive performance. Organizational strategies include providing flexible work arrangements, fostering a positive work culture, and implementing stress management programs.

Understanding the nuanced relationship between stress and performance is crucial for programmers and organizations aiming to foster environments that maximize productivity and well-being. By recognizing the dual nature of stress and implementing effective strategies to manage it, the programming community can harness the potential of stress as a catalyst for enhanced performance while mitigating its negative consequences. This balance is essential for sustaining the cognitive and emotional health of programmers in an ever-evolving technological landscape.

Motivation and Persistence

Motivation and persistence are central to the cognitive framework of a successful programmer. They form the bedrock upon which the intricate architecture of problem-solving skills is built. Without these driving forces, even the most technically proficient individual may falter in the face of complex challenges inherent in the programming domain.

Motivation, in the context of programming, can be understood as the internal drive that compels an individual to engage with coding tasks, despite their inherent complexity and potential for frustration. This motivation may originate from intrinsic sources, such as the satisfaction derived from solving puzzles or creating functional software, or extrinsic sources, like career advancement and financial incentives. Intrinsic motivation is often deemed more sustainable, as it aligns with personal interests and passions, fostering a deeper engagement with the task at hand.

The role of motivation extends beyond mere initiation of tasks. It influences the quality of cognitive engagement and the ability to sustain effort over prolonged periods. A motivated programmer is more likely to employ metacognitive strategies, such as planning, monitoring, and evaluating their work, which are crucial for effective problem-solving. Moreover, motivation can enhance resilience against setbacks, facilitating the iterative process of debugging and optimization that characterizes much of programming work.

Persistence, on the other hand, refers to the steadfastness and continuity in the pursuit of programming goals, despite challenges and obstacles. It is the unwavering commitment to see a project through to completion, regardless of the difficulties encountered along the way. Persistence is particularly crucial in programming due to the iterative nature of software development, where trial and error are integral components of the workflow.

The interplay between motivation and persistence is complex and dynamic. Motivation provides the initial impetus and energy, while persistence ensures that this energy is channeled productively over the long term. Together, they form a synergistic relationship that enables programmers to navigate the often tumultuous landscape of software development.

In cultivating motivation and persistence, several strategies can be employed. Goal setting is one such strategy, where programmers delineate clear, achievable objectives that provide a sense of direction and purpose. Regular feedback, whether from peers, mentors, or self-assessment, can also reinforce motivation by highlighting progress and areas for improvement. Furthermore, fostering an environment that encourages exploration and creativity can enhance intrinsic motivation, making the programming endeavor more enjoyable and fulfilling.

Another critical aspect is the development of a growth mindset, where challenges are viewed as opportunities for learning and development rather than insurmountable obstacles. This mindset not only bolsters persistence but also enhances the capacity for adaptive learning, enabling programmers to continuously refine their skills and knowledge in response to new challenges.

Ultimately, motivation and persistence are not static traits but dynamic processes that can be nurtured and developed over time. By understanding and harnessing these processes, programmers can enhance their cognitive resilience and problem-solving efficacy, leading to greater success and satisfaction in their professional endeavors. The psychological underpinnings of these concepts provide valuable insights into the mindset required to thrive in the ever-evolving field of programming, where challenges are not only inevitable but essential for growth and innovation.

Creativity in Problem Solving

In the realm of programming, the act of problem-solving is not merely a linear process but a complex interplay of logic, intuition, and creativity. While algorithmic precision is often heralded as the cornerstone of effective programming, the role of creativity cannot be understated. This chapter delves into the nuances of creative thinking within the context of programming, elucidating its significance and exploring methodologies that foster innovation.

Creative problem-solving in programming involves the ability to transcend conventional boundaries and approach problems with a fresh perspective. This requires a mental shift, a departure from rigid frameworks, and an openness to explore alternative avenues. The essence of creativity lies in the programmer's capacity to generate novel ideas and solutions that are not immediately evident.

One of the key aspects of creativity in programming is the ability to synthesize disparate concepts. Programmers often draw inspiration from various domains, integrating ideas from seemingly unrelated fields to forge unique solutions. This interdisciplinary approach can lead to breakthroughs that pure algorithmic thinking might not achieve. For example, concepts from biology or physics can inspire solutions in software design, leading to more efficient algorithms or innovative user interfaces.

Another crucial element is the cultivation of a mindset that embraces ambiguity and uncertainty. Programming challenges often present themselves as ill-defined problems, requiring a degree of comfort with the unknown. Creative programmers are adept at navigating these uncertainties, employing trial and error, iterative testing, and prototyping to refine their solutions. This iterative process not only enhances problem-solving skills but also encourages the discovery of unforeseen pathways and solutions.

The environment in which programming occurs also plays a pivotal role in nurturing creativity. Collaborative settings, where diverse perspectives converge, can significantly enhance creative output. Pair programming, code reviews, and brainstorming sessions foster a culture of open communication and idea exchange, which are essential for creative problem-solving. Such environments encourage programmers to challenge assumptions, question norms, and push the boundaries of traditional thinking.

Moreover, tools and technologies themselves can be catalysts for creativity. The advent of new programming languages, frameworks, and platforms provides programmers with fresh opportunities to rethink and reimagine existing solutions. These technological advancements often come with unique features and paradigms that can inspire creative approaches to problem-solving.

Developing creativity in programming also involves honing the ability to think abstractly. Abstract thinking enables programmers to conceptualize problems at a higher level, identifying patterns and structures that are not immediately apparent. This skill is crucial in designing scalable and efficient systems, as it allows programmers to distill complex problems into manageable components.

In cultivating creativity, it is essential to encourage a culture of experimentation and learning. Failure should be perceived as a stepping stone to success, an opportunity to gain insights and refine approaches. Encouraging an attitude of curiosity and a willingness to explore uncharted territories can unlock the full potential of creativity in programming.

Ultimately, creativity in problem-solving is an indispensable asset in a programmer's toolkit. It transforms the act of programming from a mechanical task into an art form, where innovation and ingenuity lead to the creation of elegant and effective solutions. By embracing creativity, programmers can not only solve problems more effectively but also contribute to the advancement of technology in profound and meaningful ways.

The Role of Passion

In the realm of programming, passion is often heralded as a critical component that separates the merely competent from the truly exceptional. Passion, in this context, can be defined as an intense enthusiasm or compelling desire to engage with the intricate challenges that programming presents. It functions not only as a motivator but as a catalyst for innovation and resilience.

The cognitive demands of programming are substantial, requiring sustained concentration, problem-solving skills, and a continuous learning mindset. Passion infuses energy into these tasks, transforming them from mundane to exhilarating endeavors. Programmers with a deep-seated passion for their craft are more likely to engage in deliberate practice, a focused and goal-oriented form of learning that is essential for mastering complex skills.

Research in cognitive psychology suggests that passionate individuals are more likely to enter a state of flow, a psychological phenomenon where one becomes fully immersed in an activity, experiencing heightened focus and enjoyment. This state is particularly conducive to programming, where prolonged periods of undistracted work can lead to significant breakthroughs and creative problem-solving.

Moreover, passion serves as a buffer against the inevitable setbacks and frustrations that come with programming. The iterative nature of coding, often characterized by trial and error, can be daunting. A passionate programmer, however, views failures not as insurmountable obstacles but as opportunities for growth. This mindset fosters resilience, enabling individuals to persist through challenges and continue refining their skills.

In addition to enhancing individual performance, passion can have a profound impact on team dynamics within programming environments. A passionate team member can inspire others, fostering a culture of enthusiasm and collaboration. This collective passion can lead to increased productivity, as team members are more willing to share ideas, experiment with novel solutions, and support one another in achieving common goals.

The role of passion in programming is further evidenced by its influence on creativity. Passionate programmers are often more willing to take risks, explore unconventional solutions, and push the boundaries of what is possible with code. This creative drive is crucial in an industry that thrives on innovation and rapid technological advancement.

However, it is important to recognize that passion must be balanced with other factors to be truly effective. While passion can drive extraordinary achievements, it can also lead to burnout if not managed properly. Programmers must learn to balance their enthusiasm with self-care practices, ensuring that their passion for coding is sustainable over the long term.

In conclusion, passion is a powerful force within the programmer's mind. It fuels motivation, enhances learning, and fosters resilience. By nurturing passion alongside other essential skills and practices, programmers can unlock their full potential, contributing to both personal success and the advancement of the field. Passion is not merely a supplement to technical skill but an integral component of a programmer's toolkit, shaping their approach to challenges and their contributions to the ever-evolving landscape of technology.

Chapter 6: The Learning Loop

Feedback Mechanisms

In the realm of programming, feedback mechanisms serve as the vital processes that allow for the adjustment and optimization of code, akin to the regulatory systems observed in biological organisms. A programmer's interaction with feedback is a continual loop of input, processing, output, and adjustment, where each iteration refines the outcome to better meet the desired objectives.

Feedback mechanisms in programming are multifaceted, ranging from self-imposed corrections during code development to external critiques from peers or automated systems. These mechanisms are essential not only for ensuring the accuracy and efficiency of code but also for fostering a mindset of continuous improvement. The iterative nature of feedback allows programmers to identify errors, optimize performance, and enhance functionality, ultimately leading to more robust and reliable software solutions.

One of the primary forms of feedback in programming is the compiler or interpreter feedback. This type of feedback is immediate and direct, providing programmers with error messages or warnings as they write code. Such real-time feedback is crucial for identifying syntax and logical errors early in the development process, thus preventing potential issues from escalating into more complex problems. Furthermore, compilers and interpreters often suggest possible corrections, guiding programmers toward best practices and more efficient coding techniques.

Another significant feedback mechanism is peer review, a process where fellow programmers evaluate and critique one's code. Peer review is instrumental in maintaining code quality, as it introduces diverse perspectives and insights, potentially uncovering issues that the original programmer may have overlooked. This collaborative feedback loop not only enhances the code itself but also promotes knowledge sharing and skill development among team members.

Automated testing frameworks represent another layer of feedback, offering a systematic approach to validating code functionality. These frameworks execute predefined test cases that simulate various scenarios, verifying that the code behaves as expected. Automated tests provide programmers with confidence in their code's reliability and performance, allowing them to make informed decisions about further development or deployment. Additionally, the feedback from automated tests can highlight areas of the code that require optimization or refactoring, contributing to the overall maintainability of the software.

The integration of continuous integration and continuous deployment (CI/CD) pipelines exemplifies the advanced application of feedback mechanisms in modern software development. CI/CD pipelines automate the process of building, testing, and deploying code, providing immediate feedback on the impact of changes. This approach minimizes the risk of introducing errors into the production environment and accelerates the development lifecycle, enabling rapid iteration and adaptation to changing requirements.

Ultimately, feedback mechanisms are integral to the programming environment, driving the evolution of code and the development of a programmer's skills. They foster an environment of accountability and precision, where each line of code is subject to scrutiny and improvement. By embracing feedback, programmers not only enhance their technical proficiency but also cultivate a mindset attuned to problem-solving and innovation. In the dynamic landscape of software development, feedback is the compass that guides programmers toward excellence, ensuring that their creations are not only functional but exemplary in their design and execution.

Adaptive Learning

Within the vast landscape of programming, the concept of adaptive learning stands as a beacon of innovation, intertwining cognitive science and technology. The essence of adaptive learning lies in its ability to tailor educational experiences to the unique needs of each learner, offering a dynamic approach to mastering programming skills.

Adaptive learning systems utilize algorithms to analyze the learner's progress and adjust content accordingly. These systems are designed to identify the strengths and weaknesses of individual programmers, providing personalized pathways that enhance learning efficiency. By continuously assessing a learner's performance, adaptive systems can present challenges that are neither too easy nor too difficult, maintaining an optimal level of engagement and motivation.

In programming education, adaptive learning can manifest in various forms. Interactive coding platforms, for instance, can adjust the complexity of exercises based on real-time assessments. If a programmer excels in a particular area, the system can introduce more complex problems to further hone their skills. Conversely, if a learner struggles, the system can offer additional resources or simpler tasks to reinforce foundational concepts.

The integration of artificial intelligence (AI) plays a pivotal role in the advancement of adaptive learning systems. AI-driven platforms can analyze vast amounts of data to predict learning patterns and outcomes, enabling the creation of highly personalized learning experiences. These platforms often incorporate machine learning algorithms that evolve over time, refining their understanding of each learner's unique trajectory.

Moreover, adaptive learning systems foster an environment of continuous feedback, a critical component in the learning process. Instant feedback mechanisms allow learners to understand their mistakes and correct them promptly, preventing the reinforcement of incorrect practices. This immediate interaction not only accelerates the learning process but also builds confidence in novice programmers as they witness tangible improvements in their skills.

The cognitive aspect of adaptive learning is rooted in the principles of metacognition—the awareness and understanding of one's own thought processes. By encouraging learners to reflect on their problem-solving strategies and outcomes, adaptive systems promote self-regulation and critical thinking. This reflective practice is essential in programming, where the ability to debug and optimize code is paramount.

Furthermore, adaptive learning environments can also facilitate collaborative learning. By analyzing data from multiple learners, these systems can identify complementary skill sets and encourage teamwork. Collaborative projects not only enhance problem-solving abilities but also prepare programmers for real-world scenarios where teamwork is often crucial.

Despite its numerous advantages, the implementation of adaptive learning in programming education is not without challenges. One of the primary concerns is ensuring the accuracy and fairness of the algorithms that drive these systems. Biases in data or algorithm design can lead to skewed learning experiences, necessitating rigorous testing and validation processes.

In the realm of programming, adaptive learning represents a paradigm shift from traditional, one-size-fits-all educational approaches. By harnessing the power of technology and data, it offers a promising pathway to cultivate a new generation of programmers equipped with the skills and confidence to thrive in an ever-evolving digital landscape. As the field continues to evolve, the potential for adaptive learning systems to transform programming education is immense, promising a future where learning is as dynamic and adaptable as the code itself.

Skill Acquisition Stages

In the domain of programming, the development of expertise is a multifaceted process characterized by the gradual transition from novice to expert. This transformation can be understood through the framework of skill acquisition stages, each delineating a distinct phase in cognitive and practical development.

Cognitive Stage

The initial stage of skill acquisition is marked by the learner's conscious engagement with new programming concepts and techniques. During this phase, individuals rely heavily on declarative knowledge—explicit facts and instructions about programming languages, syntax, and basic algorithms. The cognitive load is substantial as programmers attempt to internalize fundamental principles while grappling with the unfamiliarity of the coding environment. Errors are frequent, and problem-solving is often guided by trial and error, demanding significant mental resources. At this stage, learning is deliberate and effortful, with progress dependent on the learner's ability to comprehend and memorize rules and structures.

Associative Stage

As programmers advance, they enter the associative stage, characterized by the gradual refinement of skills through practice and the integration of declarative knowledge into procedural knowledge. The cognitive load decreases as repetitive coding tasks become more automatic, and learners begin to recognize patterns and commonalities in their work. Feedback mechanisms, whether from code editors or peer reviews, play a crucial role in this phase, helping individuals correct errors and optimize their approaches. The assimilation of knowledge allows for more efficient problem-solving, as programmers start to develop strategies for debugging and code optimization. At this stage, learners exhibit increased confidence and accuracy, although they still require conscious effort to handle complex or novel programming challenges.

Autonomous Stage

The transition to the autonomous stage signifies the attainment of expertise, where programming skills become highly automated and require minimal conscious deliberation. Programmers at this level demonstrate fluidity in their work, effortlessly navigating through complex codebases and employing advanced algorithms with ease. This stage is characterized by the ability to multitask and adapt to new problems without significant cognitive strain. The expert programmer possesses a deep understanding of programming paradigms and can intuitively apply them to diverse contexts. Moreover, problem-solving becomes a creative process, as the expert draws on a vast repertoire of experiences and solutions to innovate and optimize. The autonomous stage reflects a mastery of both the technical and conceptual aspects of programming, allowing for efficient and effective application of skills in real-world scenarios.

Through these stages, the trajectory of skill acquisition in programming underscores the importance of practice, feedback, and the gradual internalization of knowledge. Each phase builds upon the previous, fostering a robust and adaptable skill set essential for navigating the ever-evolving landscape of technology. Understanding these stages not only aids in the development of individual programmers but also informs educational strategies, enabling instructors to tailor their approaches to meet the needs of learners at different points in their journey toward expertise. By recognizing the intricacies of skill acquisition, both novice and experienced programmers can better navigate their learning paths, maximizing their potential in the dynamic field of software development.

Continuous Improvement

In the ever-evolving landscape of programming, the concept of continuous improvement is not merely a methodology but a necessity. It is an ongoing process that involves perpetual learning, adaptation, and refinement of skills, processes, and tools. For programmers, this philosophy is embedded in both the development of code and personal growth as professionals.

Continuous improvement in programming can be dissected into several facets, each contributing to the overall enhancement of both individual and team capabilities. At its core, it involves a cycle of planning, executing, reviewing, and refining. This cycle is akin to the scientific method, where hypotheses are tested, results are analyzed, and adjustments are made based on empirical evidence. Such an approach ensures that programming practices evolve in response to new challenges and insights.

One of the primary aspects of continuous improvement is the integration of feedback loops. These loops, whether they occur in the form of code reviews, automated testing, or user feedback, provide critical information that programmers can use to enhance their output. Regular code reviews, for instance, allow developers to identify potential issues and learn from each other's experiences, fostering a culture of collaboration and knowledge sharing. Automated testing, on the other hand, offers immediate feedback on code functionality, enabling quick identification and rectification of errors.

Another crucial element is the cultivation of a growth mindset. This psychological framework encourages programmers to view challenges as opportunities for growth rather than obstacles. A growth mindset fosters resilience and adaptability, qualities that are indispensable in a field characterized by rapid technological advancements. Programmers with this mindset are more likely to engage in deliberate practice, seeking out tasks that stretch their abilities and provide opportunities for learning.

Moreover, the adoption of agile methodologies in software development epitomizes continuous improvement. Agile frameworks such as Scrum and Kanban emphasize iterative progress, flexibility, and responsiveness to change. They facilitate a dynamic environment where teams can adjust their workflows based on real-time data and project requirements. This adaptability ensures that software products remain relevant and effective in meeting user needs.

Knowledge management also plays a pivotal role in the continuous improvement of programming practices. Maintaining comprehensive documentation, sharing knowledge through wikis or internal forums, and encouraging mentorship are strategies that support the dissemination and retention of expertise. These practices not only enhance individual learning but also contribute to the collective intelligence of programming teams.

Lastly, the incorporation of new technologies and tools is a cornerstone of continuous improvement. As the technological landscape evolves, programmers must remain abreast of emerging trends and innovations. This may involve learning new programming languages, adopting cutting-edge development tools, or exploring novel paradigms such as machine learning and artificial intelligence. By embracing technological advancements, programmers can enhance their productivity, improve code quality, and deliver more robust solutions.

In the context of a programmer's mind, continuous improvement is a relentless pursuit of excellence. It requires dedication, openness to change, and a commitment to lifelong learning. By embedding these principles into their professional ethos, programmers can navigate the complexities of their field with confidence and competence, ultimately advancing both their careers and the quality of the software they create.

Mastery and Expertise

Mastery in programming is not merely an endpoint but a continuous process marked by an ever-deepening understanding of both fundamental and advanced concepts. Expertise, while often perceived as an accumulation of knowledge, is better understood as the ability to apply this knowledge effectively and innovatively.

The journey to mastery demands a solid foundation in core programming principles. These principles are not limited to syntax and language-specific details but extend to algorithmic thinking, problem-solving strategies, and an understanding of computational theory. This foundational knowledge serves as the bedrock upon which further skills are built, allowing the programmer to transcend beyond mere code writing to strategic and systemic thinking.

A crucial aspect of developing expertise is the iterative process of learning and application. This involves actively engaging with new challenges, reflecting on past solutions, and integrating lessons learned into future endeavors. This reflective practice enhances cognitive flexibility, enabling programmers to adapt their approaches to suit varying contexts and problems.

Moreover, expertise is characterized by an intuitive grasp of patterns and structures within code. Experienced programmers develop a mental repository of idiomatic solutions, which they draw upon when faced with new problems. These mental models allow them to anticipate potential issues, streamline processes, and optimize performance with efficiency and precision.

A significant component of mastery involves the ability to navigate and utilize various tools and environments effectively. Mastery is not confined to a single language or framework but is instead demonstrated by the ability to quickly acclimate to new technologies and integrate them into existing workflows. This adaptability is a hallmark of true expertise, as it reflects a deep understanding of the underlying principles that govern all programming languages and tools.

The social aspect of programming should not be underestimated in the pursuit of mastery. Collaboration with peers, participation in code reviews, and engagement in community discussions facilitate the exchange of ideas and the refinement of techniques. Such interactions expose programmers to diverse perspectives and solutions, broadening their understanding and fostering innovation.

Furthermore, the role of mentorship cannot be overstated. Learning from seasoned experts provides invaluable insights that accelerate the mastery process. Mentors offer guidance not only in technical skills but also in navigating the professional landscape, cultivating a holistic approach to career development.

The pursuit of mastery also involves a commitment to lifelong learning. The technology landscape is ever-evolving, and staying abreast of the latest advancements is essential. This ongoing education can take many forms, from formal coursework to self-directed projects and experimentation.

In conclusion, mastery and expertise in programming are dynamic states, characterized by a deep understanding of foundational principles, an ability to apply knowledge creatively, and a commitment to continuous learning. They are marked by both individual and collaborative efforts, as well as an ongoing engagement with the broader programming community. This holistic approach ensures that programmers not only remain relevant in their field but also contribute meaningfully to its advancement.

Chapter 7: Collaborative Coding

Team Dynamics

The intricate architecture of a programmer's mind is akin to a finely tuned orchestra, where each player contributes to the symphony of software development. In this realm, team dynamics serve as the conductor, orchestrating harmony and coherence among diverse individuals to transform lines of code into functional, innovative products. Understanding the essence of team dynamics is paramount, as it influences productivity, innovation, and the overall success of software projects.

At the core of effective team dynamics lies communication, a fundamental pillar that bridges the gap between individual cognition and collective achievement. Programmers, often perceived as solitary thinkers, must navigate the complexities of conveying intricate ideas and technical jargon to colleagues with varying levels of expertise. The ability to articulate thoughts clearly, listen actively, and engage in meaningful dialogue fosters an environment where knowledge is shared, misconceptions are clarified, and collective problem-solving is enhanced.

In addition to communication, the diversity of thought plays a crucial role in shaping team dynamics. A team composed of members with diverse backgrounds, experiences, and skill sets can approach problems from multiple angles, leading to innovative solutions and creative breakthroughs. This diversity, however, requires careful management to prevent potential friction and to ensure that every voice is heard and valued. Cultivating an inclusive culture where diverse perspectives are embraced enhances the team's adaptability and resilience in the face of complex challenges.

Leadership within the team is another pivotal factor influencing dynamics. The role of a leader is not to dictate but to guide, inspire, and empower team members. Effective leaders set clear goals, provide constructive feedback, and create an atmosphere of trust and mutual respect. They understand the individual strengths and weaknesses of each team member and strategically assign tasks that align with their capabilities, optimizing the team's overall performance. Moreover, leaders must possess emotional intelligence to navigate interpersonal conflicts and to maintain a positive team morale.

Furthermore, the psychological safety of team members is integral to fostering an environment where individuals feel comfortable expressing their ideas and taking risks without fear of ridicule or retribution. When programmers feel safe to voice their opinions and experiment, they are more likely to contribute innovative ideas and engage in creative problem-solving. This culture of safety encourages continuous learning and adaptation, which are essential in the ever-evolving landscape of software development.

Collaboration tools and methodologies also significantly impact team dynamics. Agile methodologies, for example, emphasize iterative development, constant feedback, and flexibility, aligning well with dynamic team environments where adaptability is key. Tools that facilitate real-time collaboration, such as version control systems and communication platforms, enable seamless coordination and integration of work, minimizing misunderstandings and redundancies.

In dissecting the multifaceted nature of team dynamics, it becomes apparent that the synergy between communication, diversity, leadership, psychological safety, and collaboration tools forms the backbone of a successful programming team. Acknowledging and nurturing these elements can transform a group of individual programmers into a cohesive unit, capable of overcoming obstacles and achieving remarkable feats in the ever-competitive world of software development. The programmer's mind, when attuned to the rhythms of effective team dynamics, becomes a powerful instrument in the orchestra of technological innovation.

Communication in Code

In the realm of programming, communication is not solely confined to spoken or written language. Code itself serves as a medium of communication — a structured language that conveys instructions to machines and, by extension, to other programmers. This dual role necessitates a nuanced understanding of code as both an executable set of instructions and a narrative that communicates intent and logic.

At its core, code is a precise language with syntax and semantics, akin to natural languages. This precision is non-negotiable; even minor syntactical errors can render a program inoperative. The programmer's task is to translate abstract ideas into this rigid structure, ensuring that each line of code accurately reflects the intended function. This process demands a high level of cognitive engagement, as programmers must continuously interpret and adapt the language to fit their needs.

The communicative function of code extends beyond interaction with machines. It also serves as a vital tool for collaboration among programmers. In collaborative environments, code must be readable and maintainable. It is not enough for code to merely function; it must be understandable to others who may need to modify or extend it in the future. This requirement introduces the concept of code readability, where clarity and simplicity are paramount. Effective code is often described as "elegant," a term that reflects both its functional efficiency and its aesthetic coherence.

Comments and documentation play a crucial role in enhancing the communicative capacity of code. While code can be self-explanatory to an extent, comments provide context and rationale that may not be immediately apparent. They serve as annotations that illuminate the programmer's thought process, offering insights into the decision-making behind certain implementations. However, comments should be used judiciously; excessive or redundant comments can clutter the code, detracting from its readability.

Moreover, the choice of programming language itself can influence the communicative nature of code. Different languages have different paradigms and styles, which can affect how ideas are expressed and understood. For instance, a language that supports object-oriented programming may facilitate a different approach to problem-solving than a functional programming language. The programmer's familiarity with these paradigms can significantly impact their ability to communicate effectively through code.

In a globalized world, programming also transcends linguistic and cultural barriers. The universality of programming languages allows individuals from diverse backgrounds to collaborate seamlessly. However, cultural differences can still manifest in coding styles and practices, underscoring the need for standardization and adherence to best practices.

Ultimately, the art of communication in code is a balancing act between precision and clarity, functionality and readability. It is a skill that evolves with experience, as programmers refine their ability to articulate complex ideas succinctly. As programming languages continue to evolve, so too will the ways in which we communicate through code, pushing the boundaries of what is possible in the digital realm. This ongoing evolution underscores the dynamic nature of programming, where communication is not merely a means to an end but a fundamental aspect of the craft itself.

Conflict Resolution

In the realm of software development, conflict is an inevitable part of the collaborative process. Developers, designers, product managers, and other stakeholders often have differing opinions, priorities, and approaches to problem-solving. Understanding the nature of these conflicts and developing effective strategies for resolution is crucial to maintaining a productive and harmonious work environment.

Conflicts in programming teams can arise from various sources. One common source is technical disagreements, where team members have diverging views on the best approach to implement a feature or solve a problem. These disagreements can stem from differences in experience, knowledge, or personal preference for certain technologies or methodologies. Another source of conflict is resource allocation, where team members vie for limited resources, such as time, budget, or personnel, to prioritize their tasks or projects. Additionally, interpersonal conflicts may arise due to personality clashes, communication barriers, or differences in work styles.

To resolve conflicts effectively, it is essential for team members to adopt a systematic approach that involves open communication, empathy, and collaboration. The first step in this process is to identify and acknowledge the existence of the conflict. This requires creating an environment where team members feel comfortable expressing their concerns and perspectives without fear of retribution. Encouraging open dialogue helps in clarifying misunderstandings and identifying the root causes of the conflict.

Once the conflict is acknowledged, the next step is to facilitate a constructive discussion aimed at finding a mutually acceptable solution. This involves active listening, where each party is given the opportunity to share their viewpoints and concerns. Active listening not only helps in understanding the perspectives of others but also demonstrates respect and validation of their opinions. It is important for team members to remain objective and focus on the issue at hand, rather than personalizing the conflict.

Empathy plays a crucial role in conflict resolution. By putting oneself in another's shoes, team members can better understand the motivations and constraints faced by their colleagues. This understanding fosters a collaborative environment where individuals are more willing to compromise and work towards a common goal. Empathy also helps in diffusing tension and building trust among team members.

Collaboration is the cornerstone of effective conflict resolution. Team members should work together to brainstorm potential solutions that address the concerns of all parties involved. This collaborative effort not only leads to more innovative solutions but also enhances team cohesion and morale. It is important for the team to evaluate the feasibility and impact of each proposed solution and agree on a course of action that aligns with the overall objectives of the project.

Finally, it is essential to establish clear guidelines and protocols for conflict resolution within the team. These guidelines should outline the steps to be taken when a conflict arises and emphasize the importance of maintaining professionalism and respect throughout the process. By having a structured approach to conflict resolution, teams can minimize disruptions and ensure that conflicts are addressed promptly and effectively.

In summary, conflict resolution in programming teams requires a combination of open communication, empathy, and collaboration. By adopting a systematic approach to addressing conflicts, teams can foster a positive work environment that promotes productivity, innovation, and mutual respect.

Distributed Teams

In recent years, the paradigm of software development has undergone a transformative shift. The advent of distributed teams, enabled by advances in communication technologies and globalization, has introduced a new dynamic in the programming world. This chapter explores the implications of distributed teams on the cognitive processes of programmers and the methodologies they employ.

The core challenge of distributed teams lies in the spatial and temporal separation of team members. This separation necessitates a reliance on digital communication tools, which, while effective, lack the richness of face-to-face interactions. As a result, programmers must adeptly navigate asynchronous communication, often requiring them to refine their written communication skills and adapt to multiple time zones. The asynchronous nature of communication can lead to delays in feedback and decision-making, which, in turn, can impact the cognitive load on individual programmers. Balancing this load becomes crucial to maintaining productivity and creativity.

Another cognitive aspect worth examining is the diversity inherent in distributed teams. Team members from varied cultural and educational backgrounds bring different problem-solving approaches and cognitive styles to the table. This diversity can enhance creativity and innovation, as it allows for a broader range of perspectives. However, it also requires programmers to develop a high level of cultural competence and adaptability. Understanding and integrating diverse viewpoints can lead to more robust software solutions, but it also demands increased cognitive effort in terms of communication and collaboration.

The collaboration tools used by distributed teams, such as version control systems, project management software, and collaborative coding platforms, play a crucial role in shaping the cognitive environment of programmers. These tools not only facilitate coordination and task management but also influence the way programmers conceptualize and manage their work. For instance, the use of version control systems requires a systematic approach to code management and a clear understanding of branching and merging strategies. This demands a level of cognitive discipline and foresight, as programmers must anticipate potential conflicts and plan their work accordingly.

Furthermore, the distributed nature of these teams often necessitates a more modular approach to software design. Programmers must develop components that can be easily integrated and tested independently of other parts of the system. This modular thinking aligns with cognitive strategies that prioritize breaking down complex tasks into manageable units. However, it also requires programmers to maintain a clear mental model of the overall system architecture, ensuring that their individual contributions align with the broader project goals.

Despite these challenges, distributed teams offer significant advantages, such as access to a global talent pool and the ability to operate around the clock. For programmers, this means exposure to a wider range of skills and expertise, which can enhance their own cognitive toolkit. By leveraging the strengths of distributed teams, programmers can foster an environment of continuous learning and adaptation, crucial elements in the ever-evolving field of software development.

In conclusion, the rise of distributed teams represents a fundamental shift in the cognitive landscape of programming. By embracing the challenges and opportunities presented by this model, programmers can enhance their problem-solving abilities and contribute more effectively to the creation of innovative software solutions. The key lies in developing the cognitive flexibility and communication skills necessary to thrive in this dynamic, interconnected world.

Peer Programming

Peer programming, often referred to as pair programming, is a collaborative approach to software development where two programmers work together at one workstation. This method is notable for its ability to enhance code quality, improve communication skills, and foster an environment of continuous learning.

The core of peer programming lies in its dual roles: the driver and the navigator. The driver is responsible for writing the code, actively engaging with the keyboard and translating ideas into executable syntax. Meanwhile, the navigator observes, reviews, and guides the driver, providing feedback and suggesting improvements. This dynamic creates a continuous dialogue that not only enhances the immediate task but also builds a shared understanding of the codebase.

Research indicates that peer programming can significantly reduce the number of bugs and errors in the final product. The real-time review and instant feedback loop help identify potential issues early, often before they manifest into more significant problems. This proactive error-checking process contributes to higher-quality code and reduces the need for extensive debugging sessions post-development.

Moreover, the collaborative nature of peer programming advances problem-solving capabilities. When two minds tackle a problem together, they bring diverse perspectives and experiences, leading to innovative solutions that might not emerge when working in isolation. This synergy is particularly beneficial when addressing complex coding challenges or when working within unfamiliar domains.

Communication skills are also honed during peer programming sessions. The necessity to articulate thoughts clearly and justify coding decisions fosters an environment where programmers learn to express their reasoning more effectively. This skill is invaluable not only within the confines of code development but also in broader professional interactions.

Beyond the technical and communicative advantages, peer programming serves as an excellent training ground for less experienced developers. Novices paired with seasoned programmers gain exposure to best practices, coding conventions, and industry standards. This mentorship accelerates the learning curve, allowing junior developers to acquire skills and knowledge at a faster pace than they might through solitary study.

Despite its many benefits, peer programming is not without its challenges. The success of this approach heavily relies on the compatibility of the paired individuals. Differences in working styles, communication preferences, and technical proficiency can hinder the collaborative process. Therefore, selecting pairs with complementary skills and fostering an open, respectful environment is crucial for maximizing the effectiveness of peer programming.

In addition, peer programming requires a shift in organizational culture towards valuing collaboration and shared responsibility. Teams must embrace the idea that collective ownership of the codebase leads to superior outcomes. This cultural shift can be challenging but ultimately rewarding, as it cultivates a more cohesive and resilient development team.

In conclusion, peer programming embodies a collaborative spirit that enhances software development processes. By leveraging the strengths of both individuals involved, it not only improves code quality and efficiency but also enriches the professional growth of developers. As the landscape of programming continues to evolve, the principles of peer programming remain a cornerstone in nurturing a programmer's mind, fostering an environment of shared knowledge and continuous improvement.

Chapter 8: Ethics in Programming

Moral Dilemmas

The modern programmer, an architect of the digital realm, often finds themselves at the crossroads of technology and ethics. As artificial intelligence and machine learning algorithms become increasingly intertwined with everyday life, the choices programmers make hold significant moral weight. The decisions they undertake can impact privacy, bias, security, and freedom, raising questions that extend beyond mere technical proficiency.

One of the fundamental ethical challenges faced by programmers is the issue of data privacy. In a world where data is the new currency, programmers have unprecedented access to personal information. This access requires a delicate balance between leveraging data for technological advancement and safeguarding individual privacy. The ethical quandary arises when considering how much data should be collected, stored, and analyzed, and whether users are adequately informed and consent to such practices. Protecting user data from breaches while maintaining transparency is a constant balancing act, necessitating a nuanced understanding of ethical data management.

Bias in algorithms presents another layer of moral complexity. Algorithms, while seemingly objective, are often imbued with the biases of their creators. These biases can manifest in various ways, from facial recognition systems that perform poorly on individuals with darker skin tones to hiring algorithms that inadvertently favor certain demographic groups. The ethical responsibility lies in recognizing these biases and actively working to mitigate them. This requires programmers to engage with diverse datasets and employ fairness-aware algorithms, ensuring that the digital products they create serve all users equitably.

Security is an ever-present concern in the digital age, and programmers are at the forefront of safeguarding systems from malicious actors. The ethical implications of security extend beyond preventing data breaches to include the moral responsibility of creating secure code and systems that do not inadvertently harm users. Programmers must navigate the tension between developing robust security measures and maintaining user experience, all while anticipating potential vulnerabilities that could be exploited by cybercriminals. This requires a proactive approach, where ethical considerations are integral to the software development lifecycle.

Furthermore, the proliferation of autonomous systems and AI-driven technologies has sparked debate over accountability. When machines make decisions, who is responsible for the outcomes? Programmers, as the creators of these systems, must grapple with the moral implications of delegating decision-making to machines. This involves designing systems with built-in accountability mechanisms, ensuring that there is a clear chain of responsibility when things go awry.

The digital landscape is not devoid of ethical frameworks, but programmers must be vigilant in their application. Codes of ethics, such as those proposed by professional organizations, provide guidelines, yet they are not exhaustive. The rapid pace of technological advancement often outstrips the development of comprehensive ethical standards. Thus, programmers must cultivate a mindset of continuous ethical reflection, questioning the broader impact of their work on society.

Navigating moral dilemmas requires an interdisciplinary approach, where programmers are not only skilled in technical domains but are also versed in ethical reasoning. This interplay between technology and ethics necessitates a commitment to lifelong learning and a willingness to engage with complex moral questions. By doing so, programmers can ensure that their contributions to the digital world are not only innovative but also ethically sound, reflecting a deep understanding of the societal implications of their work.

In the evolving landscape of technology, moral dilemmas are not mere theoretical concerns but practical challenges that shape the future of digital society. As such, programmers must rise to the occasion, embracing the ethical responsibilities that accompany their pivotal role in the digital age.

Privacy Concerns

In the rapidly evolving digital landscape, where the boundaries of technology and human interaction blur, the issue of privacy emerges as a pivotal concern for programmers. The intrinsic nature of programming demands an understanding of data manipulation, storage, and transmission. However, along with these capabilities comes the responsibility to safeguard user information against misuse and unauthorized access.

The programmer's approach to privacy is multifaceted, encompassing technical, ethical, and legal considerations. At its core, the challenge lies in designing systems that respect user privacy while still delivering the desired functionality. This requires a deep understanding of data protection principles and an awareness of potential vulnerabilities inherent in software systems.

One of the primary technical challenges is the implementation of robust encryption methods. Encryption serves as the first line of defense, transforming sensitive data into unreadable formats for unauthorized users. Programmers must stay abreast of the latest cryptographic techniques and ensure that their applications adhere to these standards. Failing to encrypt data properly can lead to significant breaches, compromising user trust and exposing organizations to legal liabilities.

Beyond technical measures, ethical considerations play a significant role in the programmer's mindset. The ethical responsibility to protect user privacy extends beyond compliance with regulations. It involves a commitment to transparency and user consent, ensuring that individuals are fully informed about how their data is collected, used, and shared. This ethical stance fosters a culture of trust between the programmer and the user, essential for the long-term success of any digital product.

Legal frameworks such as the General Data Protection Regulation (GDPR) in Europe and the California Consumer Privacy Act (CCPA) in the United States provide guidelines for data privacy. These regulations impose strict requirements on organizations to protect personal data and grant users rights over their information. Programmers must be familiar with these laws, as non-compliance can result in severe penalties and damage to reputation.

The challenge of maintaining privacy is further complicated by the increasing complexity of software systems. As applications become more interconnected through APIs and third-party integrations, the potential attack surface expands. Programmers must be vigilant in assessing the security of these connections and implementing measures such as token-based authentication and secure data transmission protocols.

Moreover, the rise of machine learning and artificial intelligence introduces new dimensions to privacy concerns. These technologies often rely on vast datasets to function effectively, raising questions about data anonymization and the potential for re-identification. Programmers working in these fields must critically evaluate their data handling practices and strive to minimize privacy risks while harnessing the power of AI.

In conclusion, the programmer's role in addressing privacy concerns is both challenging and essential. By combining technical expertise with ethical responsibility and legal awareness, programmers can design systems that protect user information and maintain trust in the digital age. As technology continues to advance, the commitment to privacy must remain a central tenet in the programmer's mind. This ongoing vigilance will ensure the creation of secure, user-centric applications that respect individual privacy and uphold the integrity of the digital ecosystem.

Algorithmic Bias

In the realm of computational decision-making, algorithms serve as the architects of modern digital interactions. These mathematical constructs are instrumental in streamlining processes, enhancing efficiencies, and, ostensibly, removing the human element that can lead to errors. However, the very nature of these algorithms can inadvertently introduce a phenomenon known as algorithmic bias, where skewed outcomes arise from seemingly impartial systems.

Algorithmic bias emerges from a myriad of sources. At its core, it often stems from the data used to train these systems. Data sets, curated by humans, can carry intrinsic biases reflective of societal prejudices. When algorithms are trained on such biased data, they can perpetuate and even exacerbate these biases, leading to decisions that are unfair or discriminatory. For instance, facial recognition software has been criticized for its higher error rates in identifying individuals with darker skin tones, a direct consequence of training data predominantly consisting of lighter-skinned individuals.

Furthermore, the design of algorithms themselves can contribute to bias. The choices made by programmers in selecting variables, setting parameters, or defining objectives can inadvertently favor certain outcomes over others. These decisions, often made with the best intentions, can nonetheless reflect unconscious biases, which are subsequently encoded into the algorithm's decision-making process. This is particularly concerning in contexts such as hiring, lending, or law enforcement, where biased outcomes can have significant societal implications.

An additional layer of complexity arises from the feedback loops inherent in algorithmic systems. As algorithms make decisions, they generate new data, which is then fed back into the system. If an algorithm's initial decisions are biased, the feedback loop can reinforce and amplify these biases over time, leading to increasingly skewed outcomes. This self-perpetuating cycle can be difficult to detect and disrupt, posing a significant challenge to those seeking to ensure fairness and equity in algorithmic decision-making.

Addressing algorithmic bias requires a multifaceted approach. One critical component is the diversification of data sets. By ensuring that training data reflects a wide range of demographics and perspectives, programmers can help minimize the risk of bias. Additionally, transparency in algorithmic design and decision-making processes is crucial. By opening these processes to scrutiny, stakeholders can identify potential sources of bias and work to mitigate them.

Moreover, the development of bias detection and mitigation tools is an emerging field of research. These tools can help identify biased outcomes and provide insights into the underlying causes, enabling programmers to refine algorithms accordingly. However, these tools are not a panacea and must be used in conjunction with broader efforts to promote diversity and inclusion within the field of computer science.

Ultimately, while algorithms have the potential to enhance decision-making processes, they are not immune to the biases that pervade human society. It is incumbent upon programmers to remain vigilant, critically evaluating the data and methods they employ, and continually striving to create systems that are both effective and equitable. As the field continues to evolve, the ongoing challenge will be to harness the power of algorithms while safeguarding against the biases that can undermine their promise.

Integrity in Code

In the realm of software development, integrity is a cornerstone that underpins the efficacy and reliability of code. The concept of integrity can be dissected into multiple dimensions, encompassing ethical considerations, structural soundness, and adherence to best practices. These facets collectively ensure that the code not only functions correctly but also adheres to the moral and professional standards expected of a proficient programmer.

At the ethical level, integrity in code demands transparency, honesty, and accountability in all stages of software development. Programmers are entrusted with the responsibility of creating systems that respect user privacy, maintain data security, and deliver accurate outcomes. This ethical obligation requires developers to rigorously test their code, promptly address vulnerabilities, and avoid shortcuts that may compromise the software's integrity. Moreover, ethical integrity necessitates the avoidance of malicious code, backdoors, and any elements that could be exploited for nefarious purposes.

Structurally, integrity in code refers to the robustness and maintainability of the software. A high-integrity codebase is characterized by clear, concise, and well-documented code that is easy to understand and modify. This involves adhering to established coding standards and conventions, which promote consistency and readability. By employing modular design principles, developers can create code that is not only easier to maintain but also more resilient to changes and less prone to errors. This structural integrity ensures that the code remains functional and efficient over time, even as it evolves.

Adherence to best practices is another critical aspect of maintaining integrity in code. This involves the implementation of rigorous testing procedures, including unit tests, integration tests, and system tests, to verify that the code performs as intended under various conditions. Continuous integration and deployment practices further ensure that changes to the codebase are systematically tested and deployed, reducing the risk of introducing errors or regressions. Additionally, the use of version control systems facilitates collaboration and accountability, providing a clear history of changes and the ability to revert to previous states if necessary.

Furthermore, integrity in code encompasses the responsibility to produce work that is original and free from plagiarism. This means respecting intellectual property rights and giving proper attribution to open-source components and libraries used within the code. By acknowledging the contributions of others and building upon existing work ethically, programmers foster a culture of respect and collaboration within the software development community.

Ultimately, integrity in code is not merely a technical requirement but a reflection of the programmer's values and professionalism. It represents a commitment to quality, reliability, and ethical responsibility, ensuring that the software serves its intended purpose without compromising the trust of its users. In an increasingly digital world, where software permeates every aspect of life, the integrity of code is paramount to building systems that are not only functional but also trustworthy and ethical.

Sustainability

In the evolving landscape of software development, sustainability extends beyond environmental considerations into the realms of code longevity, resource efficiency, and ethical responsibility. The programmer's mind, attuned to these dimensions, can significantly contribute to sustainable practices in the digital world.

Code Longevity and Maintenance
The lifespan of a software product is often dictated by its codebase's sustainability. Sustainable code is characterized by its readability, modularity, and ease of maintenance. Adopting practices such as clear documentation, adherence to coding standards, and regular refactoring ensures that the code remains comprehensible and adaptable to future needs. This not only prolongs the software's usability but also reduces the need for complete rewrites, conserving resources and minimizing waste.

Resource Efficiency
Efficient use of computational resources is a critical component of sustainability in programming. By optimizing algorithms and data structures, programmers can reduce the energy consumption of software applications. This not only has a direct impact on the environmental footprint of software but also enhances performance and user experience. Techniques such as lazy loading, efficient memory management, and employing asynchronous processing can lead to significant resource savings.

Ethical Responsibility

Sustainability in programming also encompasses ethical considerations. Programmers must be mindful of the social implications of their work, ensuring that software solutions do not contribute to societal harm, such as perpetuating biases or violating privacy. Ethical programming practices involve transparent data handling, inclusive design, and the implementation of security measures to protect user data. By embedding ethical considerations into the development process, programmers can create software that responsibly serves society.

Open Source Contributions

The open-source movement exemplifies sustainability by fostering collaboration and sharing of resources. Contributing to open-source projects not only distributes the workload but also enhances the quality and reliability of software through community engagement. Open-source initiatives promote transparency and collective problem-solving, enabling sustainable development practices that benefit both developers and end-users.

Continuous Integration and Delivery

The adoption of continuous integration and delivery (CI/CD) pipelines facilitates sustainable software development by streamlining processes and reducing redundancy. Automated testing and deployment ensure that code changes are systematically verified, minimizing errors and enhancing reliability. This approach supports sustainable practices by accelerating feedback loops, reducing the time and resources required for manual testing and deployment.

Sustainable Software Design

Designing software with sustainability in mind involves considering the entire lifecycle of the application. From inception to decommissioning, sustainable design practices focus on minimizing resource usage, maximizing adaptability, and ensuring that the software can evolve with technological advancements. This holistic approach necessitates a forward-thinking mindset, anticipating future needs and potential challenges.

Educating for Sustainability

Instilling sustainability-focused values in the next generation of programmers is crucial for the continued evolution of the field. Educational programs must emphasize the importance of sustainable coding practices, resource efficiency, and ethical responsibility. By fostering an awareness of sustainability in programming curricula, we equip future developers with the tools and mindset necessary to contribute positively to the global digital ecosystem.

Sustainability in programming is a multifaceted pursuit that requires a deliberate and informed approach. By integrating sustainable practices into the fabric of software development, programmers can make meaningful contributions to a more resource-efficient and ethically responsible digital future.

Chapter 9: The Future of Programming

AI and Machine Learning

Artificial Intelligence (AI) and Machine Learning (ML) have become pivotal in transforming the landscape of technology and programming. These fields have evolved from theoretical constructs into practical tools that are reshaping industries and enhancing daily life. Understanding AI and ML is crucial for programmers to harness their potential effectively.

AI refers to the simulation of human intelligence processes by machines, particularly computer systems. These processes include learning, reasoning, problem-solving, perception, and language understanding. Machine Learning, a subset of AI, focuses on the development of algorithms that allow computers to learn from and make decisions based on data.

Machine Learning algorithms are broadly categorized into supervised, unsupervised, and reinforcement learning. Supervised learning involves training a model on a labeled dataset, where the input and output are known. The model learns to map inputs to outputs, making it suitable for tasks like classification and regression. Unsupervised learning, on the other hand, deals with unlabeled data, allowing the model to identify patterns or clusters without prior knowledge of the outcomes. Reinforcement learning involves training models through a system of rewards and penalties, enabling them to make sequences of decisions.

A fundamental aspect of AI and ML is data. The quality and quantity of data significantly influence the performance of machine learning models. Data preprocessing, which includes cleaning, normalizing, and transforming data, is a critical step in ensuring that models perform optimally. Feature engineering, the process of selecting and transforming variables to improve model accuracy, is also essential.

Neural networks, inspired by the human brain's architecture, are a cornerstone of modern AI. They consist of layers of interconnected nodes, or neurons, that process input data to produce an output. Deep learning, a subset of ML, involves neural networks with multiple hidden layers, enabling the model to learn complex representations. Convolutional Neural Networks (CNNs) and Recurrent Neural Networks (RNNs) are specialized architectures within deep learning, each suited for specific tasks like image recognition and sequence prediction, respectively.

Programming languages like Python and R have become popular in the AI and ML community due to their extensive libraries and frameworks, such as TensorFlow, PyTorch, and scikit-learn. These tools provide the necessary infrastructure to develop, train, and deploy machine learning models efficiently.

AI and ML applications are vast, ranging from natural language processing, computer vision, and autonomous vehicles to healthcare, finance, and entertainment. In natural language processing, AI models can understand and generate human language, facilitating applications like chatbots and language translation. In healthcare, AI assists in diagnosing diseases and personalizing treatment plans, while in finance, it helps in fraud detection and algorithmic trading.

The ethical considerations surrounding AI and ML are of paramount importance. Issues such as data privacy, bias in algorithms, and the impact on employment necessitate a careful approach to the development and deployment of AI systems. Programmers must be cognizant of these challenges and strive to create fair, transparent, and accountable AI solutions.

As AI and ML continue to advance, they present both opportunities and challenges. Programmers equipped with a deep understanding of these technologies are well-positioned to innovate and contribute to the evolving digital landscape, shaping the future of technology in profound ways.

Quantum Computing

The realm of quantum computing represents a paradigm shift in the field of computation, challenging the deterministic nature of classical computers. At its core, quantum computing leverages the principles of quantum mechanics, particularly superposition and entanglement, to perform calculations at unprecedented speeds and efficiencies.

A quantum bit, or qubit, is the fundamental unit of quantum information analogous to the classical bit. However, unlike a classical bit which exists in a state of either 0 or 1, a qubit can exist in a superposition of states, representing both 0 and 1 simultaneously. This characteristic enables quantum computers to process a vast amount of possibilities in parallel, dramatically enhancing computational power.

Furthermore, quantum entanglement, a phenomenon where qubits become interlinked such that the state of one qubit instantaneously influences the state of another, regardless of the distance separating them, amplifies this capability. Entangled qubits can perform complex calculations with a degree of efficiency unattainable by classical systems.

The implications of quantum computing are profound, particularly in areas such as cryptography, optimization, and drug discovery. In cryptography, the ability of quantum computers to factor large numbers exponentially faster than classical counterparts threatens the security of current encryption standards. Algorithms like Shor's algorithm exploit this potential, prompting the development of quantum-resistant cryptographic techniques.

Optimization problems, which involve finding the best solution from a vast set of possibilities, stand to benefit immensely from quantum computing. Quantum algorithms such as Grover's algorithm can search unsorted databases quadratically faster than classical algorithms, offering significant advantages in fields ranging from logistics to artificial intelligence.

In drug discovery, the simulation of molecular interactions at the quantum level provides a more accurate model of chemical processes, potentially accelerating the development of new pharmaceuticals. Quantum computers can simulate complex molecules that are currently infeasible for classical computers, offering insights into molecular behavior and interactions that can lead to groundbreaking treatments.

Despite its potential, quantum computing is still in its nascent stages. Challenges such as error rates, decoherence, and qubit scalability must be addressed to realize the full capabilities of quantum systems. Current quantum computers, often referred to as noisy intermediate-scale quantum (NISQ) devices, are limited by these factors, restricting their application to specific problems where quantum advantage is clear.

The development of quantum error correction techniques and more stable qubit designs are pivotal in overcoming these challenges. Research into topological qubits, which promise greater error resistance, and advancements in quantum algorithms continue to drive the field forward.

As quantum computing evolves, its integration with classical systems will be crucial. Hybrid models, where quantum and classical computers work in tandem, are likely to emerge, leveraging the strengths of both paradigms. This synergy may redefine the landscape of computation, offering solutions to problems that were previously deemed intractable.

For programmers, understanding the principles of quantum computing and its potential applications is essential to navigating this emerging domain. As the field expands, it will open new avenues for innovation, requiring a blend of classical programming expertise and quantum insight to harness its power effectively.

Augmented Reality

Augmented reality (AR) represents a fascinating confluence of technology and perception, wherein digital information is superimposed onto the physical world. This technological advancement enhances the user's interaction with their environment by providing additional layers of information that are seamlessly integrated into their field of view. In the realm of programming, AR presents unique challenges and opportunities, demanding an understanding of both the hardware capabilities and the software intricacies that bring this technology to life.

At its core, AR leverages a combination of sensors, cameras, and display technologies to accurately map digital objects onto real-world spaces. The primary goal is to create an illusion where virtual elements coexist harmoniously with physical surroundings. This requires robust algorithms that can process spatial data in real-time, ensuring that virtual objects maintain their position and orientation relative to the user's perspective. Consequently, programmers must be adept at utilizing computer vision techniques, including object recognition, motion tracking, and depth sensing.

In recent years, the proliferation of mobile devices with advanced processing power and sophisticated sensors has accelerated the adoption of AR. Smartphones and tablets, equipped with cameras and gyroscopes, serve as accessible platforms for AR applications. Developers can harness these capabilities through software development kits (SDKs) such as ARKit for iOS and ARCore for Android, which provide essential tools for creating immersive AR experiences. These SDKs abstract much of the complex mathematics involved in spatial computing, allowing programmers to focus on the creative aspects of application design.

The potential applications of AR are vast and varied, spanning numerous industries. In education, AR can transform learning environments by bringing abstract concepts to life, enabling interactive and engaging educational experiences. In healthcare, AR facilitates advanced visualization techniques for medical imaging, assisting practitioners in diagnosing conditions with greater precision. In retail, AR allows consumers to visualize products in their intended environment, enhancing the shopping experience and driving informed purchasing decisions.

Despite its promise, AR also presents several technical challenges. Ensuring the seamless integration of virtual and real-world elements demands high computational efficiency, particularly in terms of rendering and latency. Developers must optimize their applications to minimize the delay between user actions and system responses, as even slight discrepancies can disrupt the illusion of reality. Furthermore, the accurate registration of virtual objects within a dynamic environment requires sophisticated environmental mapping and object recognition capabilities.

Security and privacy concerns are also paramount in AR development. As AR devices continuously capture and process environmental data, safeguarding user information becomes essential. Developers must implement robust privacy protocols to prevent unauthorized access to sensitive data, ensuring that users can trust the applications they interact with.

Looking to the future, the evolution of AR will likely be driven by advancements in hardware, such as lightweight, high-resolution headsets and improved sensor technologies. As these developments unfold, programmers will continue to play a critical role in shaping the landscape of augmented reality, pushing the boundaries of what is possible and redefining the ways in which we interact with the world around us.

The Internet of Things

In the evolving landscape of modern technology, the Internet of Things (IoT) represents a transformative shift, bridging the gap between the digital and physical worlds. As programmers, our role in this ecosystem is both pivotal and challenging, requiring a deep understanding of interconnected devices and data-driven environments.

The concept of IoT revolves around the seamless integration of everyday objects with the internet, allowing them to communicate, analyze, and act upon data without human intervention. This connectivity extends beyond conventional computing devices to encompass a myriad of objects, from household appliances to industrial machinery, each equipped with sensors and software. The potential for innovation within this space is vast, offering opportunities to enhance efficiency, improve user experiences, and drive economic growth.

From a programmer's perspective, the task begins with understanding the architecture of IoT systems. These systems are typically comprised of three main components: the devices themselves, the network they communicate over, and the cloud platform where data is processed and stored. Each component presents its own set of challenges and opportunities.

The devices, or "things," are the foundation of IoT. They vary widely in complexity, from simple sensors that measure temperature or humidity, to sophisticated machines capable of processing data locally. The design and implementation of these devices require careful consideration of power consumption, data security, and interoperability. Programmers must develop efficient firmware that ensures reliable operation under varying conditions, often leveraging lightweight protocols like MQTT or CoAP.

Networking is the next critical layer, as it facilitates communication between devices and the cloud. The choice of communication protocol—whether Wi-Fi, Bluetooth, Zigbee, or a cellular network—depends on factors such as range, bandwidth, and power constraints. Ensuring robust and secure data transmission is paramount, necessitating the use of encryption techniques and secure authentication methods.

The cloud serves as the central hub for data aggregation and analysis. Here, vast amounts of data generated by IoT devices are collected and processed, enabling real-time decision-making and long-term analytics. Programmers must design scalable cloud architectures that can handle fluctuating data loads, employing technologies like serverless computing and microservices to optimize performance and cost.

Data privacy and security are critical considerations in IoT development. As devices collect sensitive information, ensuring its protection through encryption, secure storage, and stringent access controls is essential. Moreover, compliance with regulations such as the GDPR must be integrated into the design process.

The proliferation of IoT devices also necessitates the development of robust management frameworks. These frameworks enable the monitoring, updating, and maintenance of devices remotely, ensuring their continued functionality and security. Programmers play a key role in creating intuitive interfaces and automation tools that streamline these processes.

In conclusion, the Internet of Things is reshaping industries and redefining the boundaries of what is possible. As programmers, our task is to harness the power of this interconnected world, crafting solutions that are innovative, secure, and sustainable. By understanding the intricate dynamics of IoT systems, we can contribute to a future where technology seamlessly integrates into the fabric of everyday life, enhancing our capabilities and enriching our experiences.

Cybersecurity Challenges

In the ever-evolving landscape of technology, cybersecurity has emerged as a paramount concern, demanding the attention of developers, organizations, and policymakers alike. As computer systems become increasingly complex and interconnected, the array of potential vulnerabilities expands, necessitating a robust understanding of the challenges that lie ahead.

One of the primary challenges in cybersecurity is the rapid pace of technological advancement. Innovations such as the Internet of Things (IoT), artificial intelligence (AI), and cloud computing, while offering significant benefits, also introduce new security risks. The proliferation of IoT devices, for example, creates a vast network of interconnected nodes, each potentially susceptible to exploitation. Ensuring the security of these devices requires not only robust encryption protocols but also a comprehensive approach to device management and network monitoring.

Moreover, the sophistication of cyber threats continues to escalate. Attackers employ advanced techniques, such as ransomware, phishing, and zero-day exploits, to infiltrate systems and exfiltrate sensitive data. Ransomware attacks, which encrypt an organization's data and demand payment for its release, have become increasingly prevalent and costly. Phishing schemes, leveraging social engineering tactics, deceive individuals into divulging confidential information, often through seemingly legitimate communications. These evolving threats necessitate a proactive cybersecurity strategy, incorporating both technological solutions and user education.

The challenge is further compounded by the global nature of cyber threats. Attackers can operate from any location, often exploiting jurisdictional boundaries to evade prosecution. This necessitates international collaboration and the establishment of standardized cybersecurity frameworks to effectively combat these threats. Developing such frameworks requires a delicate balance between security and privacy, ensuring that protective measures do not infringe upon individual rights.

Additionally, the shortage of skilled cybersecurity professionals presents a significant barrier to effective defense. Organizations often struggle to recruit and retain individuals with the necessary expertise to identify and mitigate threats. This skills gap underscores the need for comprehensive educational programs and industry partnerships to cultivate a new generation of cybersecurity experts.

The integration of cybersecurity into the software development lifecycle is another critical area of focus. Traditional development practices often prioritize functionality and performance over security, leading to vulnerabilities that can be exploited post-deployment. The adoption of secure coding practices, coupled with rigorous testing and continuous monitoring, is essential to mitigate these risks. Embracing a "security by design" philosophy ensures that applications are built with security considerations at the forefront, reducing the potential attack surface.

Finally, the human factor remains a persistent challenge in the realm of cybersecurity. Employees, often considered the weakest link in the security chain, can inadvertently compromise systems through actions such as using weak passwords or falling victim to social engineering attacks. Cultivating a culture of cybersecurity awareness within organizations is crucial, empowering individuals to recognize and respond to potential threats effectively.

Cybersecurity challenges are multifaceted and dynamic, requiring an interdisciplinary approach that encompasses technology, policy, and human behavior. As the digital landscape continues to evolve, so too must our strategies for safeguarding the systems and data upon which we increasingly rely. Understanding and addressing these challenges is vital to protecting the integrity and confidentiality of information in an interconnected world.

Chapter 10: The Programmer's Toolkit

Essential Tools

In the realm of programming, the importance of selecting the right tools cannot be overstated. These tools form the cornerstone of a programmer's workflow, shaping the efficiency and quality of the development process. From integrated development environments (IDEs) to version control systems, the landscape of essential tools is vast and dynamic, adapting continually to meet the evolving demands of the industry.

Integrated Development Environments (IDEs) serve as the primary interface between the programmer and the code. They provide a cohesive environment where multiple tasks can be executed seamlessly. Modern IDEs offer features such as syntax highlighting, code completion, and debugging utilities, which significantly enhance productivity and reduce the likelihood of errors. Popular IDEs include Visual Studio Code, IntelliJ IDEA, and Eclipse, each offering unique features tailored to specific programming languages and development needs.

Version control systems (VCS) are indispensable in managing changes to the codebase and facilitating collaboration among developers. Systems like Git, along with platforms such as GitHub, GitLab, and Bitbucket, provide robust mechanisms for tracking modifications, branching, and merging code. These tools ensure that the integrity of the codebase is maintained, allowing multiple developers to work concurrently without conflicts. The ability to revert changes and maintain a history of the code evolution is crucial for both individual projects and large-scale software development.

Text editors, though seemingly basic, are fundamental tools for any programmer. While IDEs offer a comprehensive suite of features, text editors like Sublime Text, Atom, and Vim provide simplicity and speed. They are particularly advantageous for quick edits or when working on remote servers. The choice of text editor often boils down to personal preference, with many programmers customizing their editors with plugins and extensions to suit their specific needs.

Compilers and interpreters transform human-readable code into machine code, enabling the execution of programs. The selection of a compiler or interpreter is typically dictated by the programming language in use. For instance, GCC is widely used for C and C++ programs, whereas Python relies on its interpreter. The efficiency of these tools directly impacts the performance of the final application, making them a critical consideration in the development process.

Debugging tools are vital for identifying and resolving issues in code. They provide insights into the execution flow and state of a program, allowing developers to pinpoint the source of errors. Tools such as GDB for C/C++ and PyCharm's integrated debugger for Python are instrumental in streamlining the debugging process, enabling developers to diagnose and fix issues swiftly.

Lastly, package managers play a crucial role in managing dependencies and libraries. Tools like npm for JavaScript, pip for Python, and Maven for Java automate the installation and updating of packages, ensuring that projects are always equipped with the latest and most secure versions of dependencies.

In essence, the selection and mastery of essential tools form the bedrock of a programmer's efficiency and effectiveness. As technology continues to advance, the landscape of these tools will undoubtedly evolve, but their fundamental role in shaping the programmer's mind and workflow remains constant. Understanding and leveraging these tools is a critical step in the journey towards becoming a proficient and adaptable software developer.

Version Control

In the realm of software development, where collaboration and rapid iterations are the norm, the ability to track and manage changes to source code efficiently is indispensable. Version control systems (VCS) serve as the backbone for maintaining the integrity and history of projects, enabling developers to work concurrently without conflict.

The evolution of version control systems has brought about significant advancements in how code is managed. Early systems, like RCS and SCCS, were limited in scope, primarily focusing on individual file versioning. These systems laid the groundwork for more sophisticated tools that address the needs of modern software development environments.

Centralized version control systems (CVCS), such as CVS and Subversion, introduced the concept of a central repository. This approach allowed multiple developers to access and commit changes to a single source, but it also introduced bottlenecks. The reliance on a central server meant that users needed constant connectivity, and any failure in the central server could disrupt the entire team's workflow.

The advent of distributed version control systems (DVCS), such as Git and Mercurial, marked a paradigm shift. Unlike their centralized counterparts, DVCS allows each developer to have a complete copy of the repository, including its full history. This decentralization enhances reliability, as developers can work offline and continue to commit changes locally. When connectivity is restored, they can synchronize their changes with the central repository or other peers.

Git, in particular, has become the de facto standard in the industry due to its robustness and flexibility. Its branching model allows developers to create, manage, and merge branches with ease, facilitating parallel development and feature isolation. This capability is crucial in complex projects where multiple features are developed simultaneously.

The integration of version control with continuous integration/continuous deployment (CI/CD) pipelines further amplifies its utility. Automated testing and deployment processes can be triggered by commits, ensuring that code changes are thoroughly vetted before reaching production environments. This integration minimizes human error and accelerates the development cycle, fostering a more agile and responsive software delivery process.

Moreover, version control systems provide essential tools for resolving conflicts and reviewing code. When multiple developers modify the same portion of code, conflicts may arise that require resolution before changes can be merged. VCS tools offer mechanisms to identify, address, and document these conflicts, ensuring that the integrity of the codebase is maintained.

In collaborative environments, code review processes are facilitated through pull requests or similar mechanisms. These processes not only help catch potential issues but also foster knowledge sharing and improve code quality through peer feedback.

The choice of a version control system and its configuration can significantly impact a team's productivity and code quality. As such, understanding the nuances of different systems and their features is crucial for any software developer. Mastery of version control tools is not merely about managing code but about enhancing collaboration, ensuring traceability, and maintaining a high standard of code integrity throughout the software development lifecycle.

Integrated Development Environments

In the realm of software development, the evolution of programming tools has been pivotal in shaping the efficiency and creativity of developers. Among these tools, Integrated Development Environments (IDEs) stand as a cornerstone, offering a cohesive suite that consolidates multiple facets of programming into a singular interface. This integration streamlines the coding process, allowing programmers to channel their cognitive resources towards problem-solving rather than tool management.

An IDE typically encompasses a code editor, compiler or interpreter, debugger, and build automation tools. The code editor is the nucleus of the IDE, equipped with syntax highlighting, code completion, and error detection features that significantly enhance code readability and reduce the cognitive load on the programmer. Syntax highlighting assists in distinguishing keywords, variables, and operators through color-coding, while code completion predicts and suggests code snippets, reducing the likelihood of syntactic errors.

The compiler or interpreter within an IDE is seamlessly integrated, facilitating the immediate translation of source code into executable programs. This integration allows for real-time feedback, enabling developers to identify and rectify errors expeditiously. Coupled with the debugger, which provides a dynamic view of program execution, developers can trace logical errors and runtime issues with precision. The debugger allows for breakpoints, watch variables, and step-through execution, offering an immersive environment for iterative testing and refinement.

Build automation tools within an IDE further enhance productivity by automating repetitive tasks such as code compilation, packaging, and deployment. This automation not only accelerates the development process but also minimizes human error, ensuring consistency in builds across different environments. Moreover, version control systems integrated within IDEs facilitate collaborative development, allowing multiple programmers to work concurrently on a project while maintaining a coherent codebase.

Beyond these core functionalities, modern IDEs are equipped with advanced features such as code refactoring tools, which assist in restructuring existing code without altering its external behavior. This capability is crucial in maintaining code quality and adaptability, allowing for the evolution of software systems in response to changing requirements. Additionally, the integration of testing frameworks within IDEs promotes a test-driven development approach, encouraging developers to validate their code against predefined test cases systematically.

The graphical user interface (GUI) of an IDE plays a vital role in enhancing user experience, offering an intuitive layout that simplifies navigation between different components. Customizable interfaces allow developers to tailor the environment to their preferences, optimizing their workflow and reducing cognitive friction. Furthermore, the extensibility of IDEs, through plugins and extensions, allows for the incorporation of additional tools and languages, catering to the diverse needs of the programming community.

While IDEs have become indispensable in modern software development, they are not without their challenges. The complexity and resource demands of IDEs can be a barrier for novice programmers and those working on lightweight projects. However, as the landscape of software development continues to evolve, the adaptability and comprehensive nature of IDEs ensure their continued relevance in nurturing a programmer's mind, facilitating the translation of abstract algorithms into tangible applications. As developers navigate the intricate world of coding, IDEs provide a structured environment that fosters innovation, collaboration, and efficiency, embodying the convergence of technology and human intellect.

Libraries and Frameworks

In the realm of software development, libraries and frameworks serve as instrumental tools that enhance the efficiency and effectiveness of programming endeavors. These components are quintessential in the modern programmer's toolkit, offering pre-written code that facilitates the development process by abstracting complex functionalities into manageable modules.

Libraries are collections of pre-compiled routines that a program can use. They encapsulate functionalities that are reusable across multiple programs, thus promoting code reusability and modularity. Libraries are typically focused on specific tasks, such as data manipulation, graphics rendering, or network communication, and can be integrated into projects as needed. The use of libraries allows developers to focus on the unique aspects of their projects by leveraging existing solutions to common problems.

Frameworks, on the other hand, offer a more comprehensive scaffold for application development. They provide a structured environment in which developers can build applications, defining the architecture and flow of the project. Unlike libraries, where the developer calls upon specific functions, frameworks often call upon the developer's code at predefined points, which is commonly referred to as "inversion of control." This characteristic of frameworks ensures that applications adhere to a consistent architecture, which can be advantageous in maintaining large-scale projects.

The distinction between libraries and frameworks is not merely semantic but also reflects their roles in shaping the software development process. Libraries afford developers the flexibility to select only the functionalities they require, integrating them into their codebase as they see fit. Frameworks, however, impose a particular structure and dictate the flow of the application, which can expedite development by providing a coherent, predefined blueprint.

The choice between using a library or a framework often depends on the scope and requirements of the project. Libraries are ideal for projects where developers seek flexibility and control, enabling them to craft bespoke solutions by assembling various components. Frameworks are more suited for projects where rapid development and adherence to a specific architecture are paramount, offering a cohesive environment that streamlines the development process.

In contemporary programming, the proliferation of open-source libraries and frameworks has democratized access to sophisticated tools, allowing developers to build complex applications with relative ease. This has led to the emergence of vibrant ecosystems around popular frameworks and libraries, fostering collaboration and innovation within the developer community.

Furthermore, the integration of libraries and frameworks into development workflows often necessitates a thorough understanding of their underlying principles and constraints. Developers must navigate documentation, understand dependencies, and ensure compatibility with other components of their projects. This requires a cognitive shift from merely writing code to orchestrating a symphony of components, each contributing to the overall functionality of the application.

The strategic use of libraries and frameworks can significantly enhance the productivity and quality of software development. By abstracting repetitive tasks and providing robust architectures, they empower developers to focus on crafting innovative solutions and addressing the unique challenges of their projects. As such, libraries and frameworks are indispensable in the programmer's arsenal, catalyzing the creation of sophisticated, scalable, and maintainable software applications.

Testing and Debugging

Software development is an intricate process, where the pursuit of perfection is often challenged by the inherent complexity of programming. Testing and debugging emerge as pivotal components in this endeavor, serving as the guardians of code reliability and functionality. The disciplined application of these processes ensures that software not only meets its requirements but also operates free of defects.

Testing, in its essence, is the systematic evaluation of software to detect discrepancies between expected and actual outcomes. It encompasses a variety of methodologies, each tailored to uncover specific types of faults. Unit testing, for instance, focuses on individual components, verifying their behavior in isolation. This granular approach allows developers to identify faults early in the development cycle, reducing the cost and effort required for rectification.

Integration testing, on the other hand, examines the interplay between components. It seeks to uncover defects that may arise from the interaction of individual units. By simulating real-world scenarios, integration testing provides a comprehensive assessment of the system's coherence and robustness.

System testing elevates the process to a holistic level, evaluating the software's compliance with the specified requirements. This phase often involves stress tests, performance assessments, and security evaluations, ensuring the software can withstand the rigors of its intended environment.

While testing aims to identify defects, debugging is the process of diagnosing and correcting these anomalies. Debugging requires a methodical approach, combining analytical reasoning with technical proficiency. The initial step involves the reproduction of the defect, which is often the most challenging aspect. Once the defect is consistently reproducible, developers proceed to isolate its source.

Isolation involves narrowing down the potential causes of the defect. Techniques such as binary search, where the code is systematically divided and tested, can expedite this process. Once the root cause is identified, corrective measures are implemented, followed by retesting to ensure the defect's resolution.

The iterative nature of debugging is worth noting. Many defects are symptomatic of deeper issues, necessitating multiple cycles of correction and testing. This underscores the importance of maintaining comprehensive documentation throughout the process, facilitating communication and collaboration among development teams.

Moreover, the advent of automated testing tools has revolutionized the landscape of testing and debugging. These tools not only accelerate the process but also enhance its accuracy, enabling developers to focus on more complex challenges. However, the reliance on automation must be tempered with human oversight, as the nuances of programming often elude algorithmic scrutiny.

In the broader context of software development, testing and debugging are indispensable. They embody the commitment to quality and reliability, underpinning the functionality of modern software systems. By embracing these processes, developers not only refine their craft but also contribute to the advancement of technology as a whole.

The meticulous application of testing and debugging is a testament to the programmer's dedication, ensuring that each line of code functions as intended. It is a pursuit that, while fraught with challenges, ultimately leads to the creation of software that is both dependable and innovative. Through this lens, one can appreciate the profound impact that these processes have on the field of programming and beyond.

Chapter 11: The Art of Refactoring

Code Readability

In the vast landscape of software development, code readability stands as a cornerstone for fostering collaboration, ensuring maintainability, and facilitating efficient debugging. The significance of readable code transcends the boundaries of individual projects, influencing the broader ecosystem in which software evolves.

Code readability is the degree to which code can be easily understood by humans. It is not merely a matter of aesthetics but a fundamental aspect that impacts the functionality and longevity of software systems. When code is readable, it allows developers to quickly grasp the logic and structure of a program, enabling them to make informed decisions about modifications, enhancements, or debugging.

The principles of code readability encompass several key elements, including clarity, consistency, and simplicity. Clarity in code is achieved by using descriptive variable and function names that convey the purpose and function of the code segments they represent. This practice reduces cognitive load and minimizes the need for excessive comments, as the code itself becomes self-explanatory.

Consistency is another pivotal factor. It involves adhering to a coherent set of coding conventions, whether they be language-specific guidelines or team-agreed standards. Consistent code style aids in maintaining uniformity across different sections of a codebase, making it easier for developers to navigate and understand. This uniformity is particularly beneficial in collaborative environments where multiple developers contribute to the same project.

Simplicity in code is crucial for readability. Complex logic and convoluted constructs can obfuscate the intent of the code, leading to increased difficulty in comprehension and higher chances of introducing errors during modifications. Simple, straightforward code, on the other hand, is easier to read, test, and maintain. This simplicity often involves breaking down complex tasks into smaller, manageable functions or methods that are easier to understand and test individually.

Moreover, code readability is inherently linked to the cognitive processes involved in reading and understanding code. Studies suggest that code reading is akin to reading natural language, requiring similar cognitive skills.

Therefore, code that mimics natural language structures can be more readily comprehensible. This involves using idiomatic expressions and leveraging the syntactic constructs of the programming language to express ideas succinctly and clearly.

The implications of code readability extend beyond individual comprehension. Readable code ensures that knowledge is preserved within the codebase, reducing the reliance on external documentation which may become outdated or incomplete. It also facilitates onboarding of new team members, allowing them to become productive more quickly by understanding the existing codebase with minimal guidance.

In essence, investing in code readability is an investment in the future of software development. It is a practice that enhances the sustainability of software projects, ensuring that they remain robust and adaptable in the face of evolving requirements and technological advancements. By prioritizing readability, developers not only improve the quality of their code but also contribute to a culture of clarity and precision that benefits the entire software development community.

Thus, as we delve deeper into the intricacies of programming, the pursuit of readable code remains a fundamental endeavor, shaping the way we write, understand, and interact with code in our ever-evolving technological landscape.

Simplifying Complexity

At the heart of programming lies the intrinsic challenge of managing complexity. This challenge, much like the art of solving a puzzle, requires both a strategic mindset and a deep understanding of the tools at hand. The essence of programming is not merely in writing lines of code but in constructing an architecture that can gracefully handle intricate and multifaceted problems.

To simplify complexity, one must first dissect the problem into manageable components. This approach, often referred to as modularization, allows a programmer to break down a large problem into smaller, more comprehensible sections. Each module can then be developed, tested, and refined independently, reducing the cognitive load and minimizing potential errors. This method not only aids in clarity but also enhances maintainability, as each module can be updated without affecting the entire system.

Abstraction is another powerful tool in the programmer's arsenal. By creating layers of abstraction, programmers can hide the underlying complexities and expose only what is necessary for each level of interaction. This promotes a cleaner, more intuitive interface, allowing developers to focus on higher-level problem-solving without being bogged down by the intricacies of lower-level operations. Abstractions are foundational in developing software libraries and APIs, which provide a simplified interface to complex functionalities.

Design patterns offer a proven pathway to tackling common problems in software development. These patterns, distilled from years of collective experience, provide templates that can be adapted to fit specific needs, offering a shortcut to effective solutions. By leveraging design patterns, programmers can avoid reinventing the wheel, instead applying tested solutions to recurring challenges. This not only speeds up development but also ensures a level of reliability and efficiency.

The principle of separation of concerns further aids in managing complexity. By delineating distinct aspects of a program, such as data handling, user interface, and business logic, programmers can isolate areas of change. This separation allows for parallel development, where teams can work on different components simultaneously, thus accelerating the development process while minimizing interdependencies.

Automation is another key strategy in simplifying complexity. Through automation, repetitive tasks can be relegated to machines, freeing up valuable human resources for more creative and analytical work. Continuous integration and continuous deployment (CI/CD) pipelines exemplify automation in action, where code is automatically tested and deployed, ensuring that the software remains in a deployable state at all times.

In this ever-evolving landscape, the ability to simplify complexity is not just advantageous; it is essential. As new technologies emerge and systems grow increasingly intricate, the demand for clear, efficient, and robust solutions will only intensify. The programmer's mind must be attuned to these demands, equipped with the skills and strategies to navigate the labyrinth of modern software development.

Ultimately, the art of simplifying complexity requires a balance between creativity and discipline. It is an ongoing pursuit, one that challenges the programmer to continually refine their approach, adapt to new paradigms, and strive for elegance in design. In mastering this skill, programmers not only enhance their own capabilities but also contribute to the creation of software that is both powerful and accessible.

Code Optimization

In the realm of software development, code optimization stands as a critical practice aimed at enhancing the performance, efficiency, and resource utilization of computer programs. This subchapter delves into the methodologies and principles that underpin the optimization of code, offering insights into both high-level strategies and low-level techniques.

Optimization is an iterative process that involves analyzing and refining code to achieve specific performance goals. It is imperative to acknowledge that optimization should not be an end in itself but rather a means to achieve efficiency without compromising the correctness and maintainability of the codebase. The balance between optimization and readability is a delicate one, where premature optimization can often lead to complex code that is difficult to maintain.

At the outset, profiling and benchmarking are essential tools for identifying bottlenecks within the code. Profiling involves measuring the performance of a program, typically by using specialized tools to gather data on execution time, memory usage, and CPU cycles. This data is invaluable in pinpointing areas where performance improvements can be made. Benchmarking, on the other hand, involves running a set of predefined tests to measure the performance of a program under specific conditions, providing a baseline against which optimizations can be evaluated.

Once the problematic areas have been identified, the process of optimization can commence. High-level optimization strategies often involve algorithmic improvements, where the choice of data structures and algorithms can have a profound impact on performance. For instance, replacing a linear search algorithm with a binary search can significantly reduce the time complexity of search operations. Similarly, choosing the appropriate data structure, such as a hash table over a linked list, can improve access and manipulation times.

At a lower level, optimization may involve code refactoring and the elimination of redundant operations. Loop unrolling, for instance, is a technique that reduces the overhead of loop control by increasing the number of operations performed per iteration. Inlining functions is another technique that eliminates the overhead of function calls by embedding the function code directly at the call site, thereby reducing execution time.

Memory management is another critical aspect of code optimization. Efficient memory allocation and deallocation, minimizing memory leaks, and reducing fragmentation can lead to significant performance gains. Techniques such as object pooling, where a set of initialized objects is kept ready for use, can reduce the overhead of frequent memory allocation and deallocation.

Parallelization and concurrency are advanced optimization techniques that leverage modern multi-core processors to improve performance. By dividing a task into smaller, concurrent sub-tasks, programs can make better use of available processing power, reducing execution time. However, this approach necessitates careful management of shared resources to avoid issues such as race conditions and deadlocks.

While optimization can yield substantial performance benefits, it is crucial to approach it with a methodical mindset. Prioritizing optimizations that offer the most significant impact with minimal code complexity is key. Moreover, maintaining thorough documentation and ensuring that optimized code remains understandable and maintainable are essential practices that support long-term code health and team collaboration.

Legacy Code Challenges

Navigating the intricate landscape of legacy code presents a formidable challenge within the realm of software development. Legacy code, often defined as code inherited from the past with outdated or obsolete structures, can become a significant hurdle for developers seeking to innovate and maintain systems efficiently. The complexity is not solely rooted in the code itself but extends to the broader context of evolving technologies, shifting paradigms, and the perpetual march of innovation.

One of the primary challenges in dealing with legacy code is the lack of comprehensive documentation. Often, the original developers have long since moved on, leaving behind scant records of their architectural decisions and coding rationales. This absence of documentation necessitates a time-consuming process of code examination and reverse engineering to discern the underlying logic and purpose of the existing structures.

The codebase's architecture can also present significant obstacles. Legacy systems were frequently developed under different paradigms and constraints than those prevalent today. As software development practices evolve, so too do the design patterns and architectural principles that guide them. This divergence can result in legacy systems that are poorly aligned with modern standards, making integration with contemporary technologies cumbersome and fraught with compatibility issues.

Moreover, legacy code is often intertwined with outdated libraries and frameworks, many of which are no longer supported. This dependency on obsolete components can introduce security vulnerabilities and performance bottlenecks, further complicating the task of maintaining and updating the system. The absence of support for these components necessitates the creation of custom solutions or the arduous task of refactoring the code to align with current technologies.

Testing legacy code presents another layer of complexity. Many legacy systems lack comprehensive test suites, making it challenging to ascertain the impact of modifications and updates. Implementing a robust testing framework requires a meticulous understanding of the system's intricacies, yet it is crucial for ensuring that changes do not inadvertently introduce new bugs or compromise system stability.

Additionally, the cultural and organizational aspects of dealing with legacy code are not to be underestimated. Developers often face resistance to change from stakeholders who may view the existing system as tried and tested. Convincing these stakeholders of the necessity for refactoring or reengineering efforts requires a delicate balance of technical acumen and persuasive communication.

Despite these challenges, the process of working with legacy code is not without its rewards. It offers developers the opportunity to delve into the history of software development, gaining insights into past methodologies and learning from the successes and failures of predecessors. Moreover, successfully modernizing a legacy system can lead to significant performance gains, enhanced security, and increased system longevity, ultimately proving the endeavor worthwhile.

In addressing legacy code challenges, a strategic approach is paramount. This involves prioritizing critical areas for refactoring, implementing incremental changes, and fostering a culture of continuous improvement. By embracing these principles, developers can transform legacy systems into robust, adaptable, and future-proof solutions that continue to serve their intended purpose in an ever-evolving technological landscape. The task demands not only technical expertise but also patience, resilience, and a forward-thinking mindset that anticipates future needs while respecting the past.

Continuous Refactoring

In the realm of software development, the construct of continuous refactoring emerges as a pivotal concept that underscores the dynamic nature of programming. It is the process of systematically improving the internal structure of code without altering its external behavior. This practice is integral to maintaining code quality and adaptability, ensuring that a software system can evolve in response to changing requirements and technology landscapes.

The philosophy of continuous refactoring is grounded in the principle of incremental improvement. By regularly revisiting and refining code, developers can address technical debt—a cumulative burden that accrues as quick fixes and shortcuts are taken to meet immediate deadlines. Over time, technical debt can lead to increased complexity and reduced maintainability, thereby hindering future development efforts. Continuous refactoring mitigates these risks by promoting a culture of ongoing enhancement and optimization.

A fundamental aspect of continuous refactoring is its reliance on a robust suite of automated tests. These tests serve as a safety net, providing assurance that changes made during the refactoring process do not inadvertently introduce defects. Test-driven development (TDD) is often employed in conjunction with continuous refactoring, as it encourages developers to write tests before implementing new functionality. This approach not only facilitates the detection of errors early in the development cycle but also reinforces the habit of refining code as it evolves.

The practice of continuous refactoring is not solely a technical exercise; it also embodies a mindset that values clarity and simplicity. Developers are encouraged to question the efficacy of their code, seeking opportunities to enhance readability and reduce complexity. This often involves breaking down monolithic functions into smaller, more manageable components, or adopting design patterns that promote flexibility and reuse. Such efforts contribute to a codebase that is easier to understand, modify, and extend.

Moreover, continuous refactoring fosters a collaborative environment where team members can engage in constructive dialogue about code quality. Code reviews become a forum for sharing insights and best practices, with refactoring serving as a catalyst for knowledge transfer and skill development. By cultivating an atmosphere of open communication and mutual respect, teams can collectively strive toward a shared vision of excellence.

It is noteworthy that continuous refactoring is not an endpoint but a perpetual process. As technology evolves and new paradigms emerge, the demands placed on software systems invariably change. Continuous refactoring equips developers with the tools and mindset needed to adapt to these changes, ensuring that their code remains relevant and robust. This adaptability is particularly crucial in an era characterized by rapid technological advancement and shifting user expectations.

In essence, continuous refactoring is an embodiment of the agile principle of responsiveness to change. It champions the idea that software development is an iterative journey, where the pursuit of perfection is balanced with the pragmatism of delivering functional solutions. By embracing continuous refactoring, developers can create software that is not only functional but also resilient, capable of withstanding the test of time and the rigors of an ever-evolving digital landscape.

Chapter 12: Understanding User Experience

User-Centered Design

In the realm of software development, the concept of user-centered design (UCD) emerges as a pivotal methodology that places the user at the forefront of the design and development process. This approach is predicated on the understanding that software should not merely function as a technical solution, but must also cater to the nuanced needs and preferences of its end users. By integrating the perspectives and feedback of users throughout the development cycle, UCD aims to enhance user satisfaction and ensure that the final product is both intuitive and efficient.

Central to user-centered design is the iterative process of engaging with users to gather insights and refine the product. This begins with an in-depth analysis of the target audience to comprehend their behaviors, challenges, and expectations. Techniques such as interviews, surveys, and observational studies are employed to create detailed user personas. These personas serve as archetypal representations of the user base, providing valuable context that guides the design process.

Once the user personas are established, the design phase commences with the creation of prototypes. These prototypes, ranging from low-fidelity sketches to interactive models, are instrumental in visualizing the user interface and user experience. They facilitate early detection of usability issues and allow for rapid adjustments based on user feedback. This stage is characterized by frequent testing and iteration, ensuring that the design evolves in response to actual user interactions rather than assumptions.

A crucial aspect of UCD is the emphasis on usability testing, which involves observing real users as they interact with the product. This testing is conducted in controlled environments where users are asked to complete specific tasks while designers and developers observe their behavior. The insights gained from these sessions are invaluable, revealing potential pain points and areas for improvement. By addressing these issues early, the development team can make informed decisions that enhance the product's usability and accessibility.

Moreover, user-centered design advocates for a holistic approach that considers the entire user journey, extending beyond the immediate interaction with the software. This encompasses understanding the context in which the product will be used and anticipating future needs. By adopting this comprehensive perspective, developers can create solutions that not only meet current user demands but also accommodate evolving requirements.

The implementation of user-centered design requires a collaborative effort across various disciplines. It necessitates the involvement of designers, developers, product managers, and stakeholders, each contributing their expertise to ensure that the user's voice is heard and prioritized. This collaborative ethos fosters a culture of empathy and innovation, driving the creation of products that are not only functional but also resonate with users on a personal level.

In adopting a user-centered design approach, developers are tasked with balancing technical possibilities with human-centered considerations. It challenges them to think beyond the code and engage with the human elements of software design. By embracing this paradigm, software development transcends its traditional boundaries, evolving into a discipline that harmonizes technology with the intricacies of human experience. Through the lens of user-centered design, the programmer's mind becomes attuned to the art of creating meaningful and impactful user experiences.

Accessibility

In the realm of programming, accessibility transcends mere compliance with guidelines; it is a foundational principle that shapes how developers approach the creation of software. As technology becomes increasingly integrated into daily life, ensuring that digital environments are accessible to all users is not only a moral imperative but also a critical component of robust software design.

Accessibility in programming involves designing and developing software applications that are usable by people with a wide range of abilities and disabilities. This includes individuals with visual, auditory, motor, or cognitive impairments. The objective is to provide a seamless and inclusive experience, ensuring that all users can effectively interact with software without encountering barriers.

A programmer's mindset towards accessibility begins with understanding the diverse needs of users. This understanding requires a comprehensive approach, encompassing both the technical and human aspects of software design. At the core is the principle of universal design, which advocates for products and environments to be inherently accessible to the widest possible audience, regardless of individual ability.

From a technical standpoint, programmers must be well-versed in accessible design practices. This includes knowledge of assistive technologies such as screen readers, alternative input devices, and speech recognition software. Programmers should ensure compatibility with these technologies by adhering to established accessibility standards and guidelines, such as the Web Content Accessibility Guidelines (WCAG). These standards provide a framework for designing software that is perceivable, operable, understandable, and robust.

Perceivability involves ensuring that all users can perceive the information presented. This might involve providing text alternatives for non-text content, such as images and videos, or ensuring that the contrast between text and background is sufficient for users with visual impairments. Operability requires that users can navigate and interact with the software, which could involve implementing keyboard shortcuts or designing intuitive touch interfaces for users with motor impairments.

Understandability focuses on making the software's interface and information easy to comprehend. This may involve using clear and simple language, providing instructions and feedback that are easy to follow, and ensuring that the software behaves in predictable ways. Robustness refers to the software's ability to function across a wide range of technologies, including older assistive devices, ensuring long-term accessibility.

Beyond technical considerations, accessibility in programming is also about fostering an inclusive design culture. This involves empathy and a commitment to understanding the experiences of users with disabilities. Programmers should engage with diverse user groups during the design and testing phases to gather feedback and insights that inform the development process.

Moreover, accessibility is not a one-time effort but an ongoing commitment. As technology evolves, so too do the needs and expectations of users. Programmers must remain vigilant, continuously assessing and updating their software to accommodate new standards and technologies. This proactive approach ensures that accessibility remains at the forefront of software development.

In conclusion, accessibility is a critical aspect of the programmer's mind. It requires a holistic approach that integrates technical skills with a deep understanding of user diversity. By prioritizing accessibility, programmers not only enhance the usability of their software but also contribute to a more inclusive digital world, where technology serves and empowers all individuals.

Performance and Usability

The intricate balance between performance and usability is pivotal in the realm of software development, particularly when viewed through the lens of a programmer's cognitive framework. At the core of this balance lies the programmer's ability to optimize software systems while ensuring that end-users experience a seamless and intuitive interaction.

Performance, in the context of programming, refers to the efficiency with which software executes tasks. This encompasses factors such as speed, resource utilization, and scalability. A programmer must rigorously analyze algorithms, data structures, and system architectures to enhance these aspects. The cognitive load involved in this process is substantial, demanding a deep understanding of computational complexity and the ability to foresee potential bottlenecks.

Usability, conversely, focuses on the user's experience with the software. It is a measure of how easily and effectively users can accomplish their goals within the system. This involves an intricate understanding of human-computer interaction principles, user interface design, and accessibility considerations. A programmer's mind is often tasked with translating complex technical functionalities into intuitive user experiences, a process that requires empathy and a keen awareness of human cognitive behaviors.

A programmer's mind must navigate the tension between these two domains. Enhancing performance can sometimes lead to increased complexity, potentially diminishing usability. Conversely, prioritizing usability might necessitate compromises in performance, such as employing higher-level abstractions that incur additional computational overhead. The challenge lies in crafting solutions that achieve an optimal balance, where the performance enhancements do not detract from usability, and vice versa.

To address this challenge, programmers frequently employ profiling and testing tools to gather empirical data on software performance. These tools allow for the identification of inefficiencies and the quantification of performance gains from various optimizations. Concurrently, usability testing, often involving user feedback and heuristic evaluations, informs the iterative refinement of the user interface and interaction patterns.

A programmer's cognitive processes during these tasks are marked by a dynamic interplay between analytical reasoning and creative problem-solving. Analytical reasoning is critical in dissecting performance metrics and understanding the underlying causes of inefficiencies. Creative problem-solving, on the other hand, is essential when devising innovative solutions that enhance usability without compromising performance.

The iterative nature of software development further complicates the programmer's task. As new features are added, both performance and usability must be reevaluated, necessitating a continuous cycle of optimization and refinement. This iterative process demands resilience and adaptability, as programmers must constantly update their mental models to accommodate new insights and technological advancements.

In conclusion, the pursuit of an ideal balance between performance and usability is a defining characteristic of a programmer's mindset. It requires not only technical expertise but also a profound understanding of human factors in computing. By mastering this balance, programmers contribute to the creation of software that is both powerful and accessible, thereby advancing the field and enhancing the user experience. This dual focus is essential for the development of software systems that are both efficient in execution and delightful to use, embodying the pinnacle of programming excellence.

Feedback Loops

In the realm of programming, feedback loops serve as a fundamental mechanism for refining code, optimizing algorithms, and enhancing user experience. These loops are integral to the iterative process that characterizes software development, enabling programmers to continuously improve their work through systematic evaluation and adjustment.

Feedback loops can be categorized into two primary types: internal and external. Internal feedback loops occur within the code itself, often through automated testing and debugging processes. Programmers utilize these loops to identify errors, optimize performance, and ensure that the code meets specified requirements. Automated testing frameworks, such as unit tests, provide immediate feedback by verifying that individual components of the code function as intended. This immediate feedback is crucial for maintaining code integrity and preventing the propagation of errors throughout the program.

External feedback loops involve input from users or stakeholders, providing insights into the program's usability, functionality, and overall effectiveness. User feedback can be gathered through various methods, including surveys, usability testing, and direct user interaction. This feedback is invaluable for understanding how the program performs in real-world scenarios and identifying areas for improvement. By incorporating user feedback into the development process, programmers can create software that better aligns with user needs and expectations.

The concept of feedback loops is deeply rooted in the scientific method, where hypotheses are tested, results are analyzed, and conclusions are drawn to refine the hypothesis further. In programming, feedback loops function similarly by allowing developers to make data-driven decisions based on empirical evidence. This evidence-based approach reduces the likelihood of introducing new errors and ensures that changes are grounded in objective analysis rather than intuition alone.

Moreover, feedback loops are instrumental in fostering a culture of continuous improvement within development teams. By regularly reviewing feedback and making iterative adjustments, teams can cultivate a mindset focused on growth and learning. This iterative approach not only enhances the quality of the software but also contributes to the professional development of programmers, as they learn to adapt and respond to new challenges.

The implementation of effective feedback loops requires careful consideration of several factors. First, the feedback must be timely and relevant, providing actionable insights

174

that can be used to drive improvements. Second, the feedback mechanisms should be designed to minimize cognitive load on developers, allowing them to focus on problem-solving rather than being overwhelmed by excessive information. Finally, feedback loops should be integrated into the development workflow in a manner that encourages collaboration and open communication among team members.

In conclusion, feedback loops are a vital component of a programmer's toolkit, enabling the continuous refinement and enhancement of software. By leveraging both internal and external feedback mechanisms, programmers can develop robust, user-centric applications that meet the evolving demands of the digital landscape. As the field of programming continues to evolve, the role of feedback loops in driving innovation and excellence remains paramount, underscoring their importance in the development of a programmer's mind.

Aesthetic Design

The intersection of programming and aesthetics is a domain where logic meets creativity, offering a unique platform for developers to express their artistry through code. Aesthetic design in programming transcends mere functionality, reaching towards a harmonious blend of performance and visual appeal. This chapter delves into the principles and practices that enable programmers to infuse their work with an aesthetic dimension that enhances user experience and engagement.

In the realm of user interfaces, aesthetics play a pivotal role. The visual layout, color schemes, typography, and spatial organization of elements all contribute to the overall user experience. A well-designed interface is not only pleasing to the eye but is also intuitive and efficient. It guides the user seamlessly through tasks, reducing cognitive load and enhancing productivity. The principles of balance, contrast, alignment, repetition, and space are key to achieving this harmony.

Balance refers to the distribution of visual weight across a design. Symmetrical balance conveys a sense of stability and order, while asymmetrical balance can create interest and dynamic tension. Contrast, on the other hand, involves the juxtaposition of differing elements to create visual interest and focal points. This can be achieved through variations in color, size, or shape.

Alignment ensures that the elements in a design are visually connected, creating a cohesive look. Proper alignment can lead to a clean and organized presentation, which is essential in maintaining the user's focus. Repetition involves the consistent use of elements such as colors, shapes, and fonts, which helps to reinforce brand identity and create a sense of unity. Finally, the strategic use of space, or negative space, is crucial in preventing designs from feeling cluttered, allowing the elements to breathe and stand out.

Beyond the visual, aesthetic design in programming also encompasses the elegance of the code itself. Code aesthetics is about writing code that is not only functional but also clean, readable, and maintainable. This involves following best practices such as adhering to coding standards, utilizing meaningful variable names, and employing consistent indentation and formatting. Such practices enhance the legibility of the code, making it easier for others to understand and modify.

Aesthetic design also considers the accessibility and inclusivity of software. Ensuring that applications are usable by people with varying abilities is a crucial aspect of design. This involves considering color contrast ratios for those with visual impairments, providing alternative text for images, and ensuring that navigation is possible using a keyboard.

Incorporating aesthetic design into programming requires a multidisciplinary approach, combining knowledge from fields such as psychology, graphic design, and human-computer interaction. It challenges programmers to think beyond the algorithm and consider the human element in their creations. This synthesis of logic and creativity not only enhances the functionality of software but also enriches the user experience, making technology more approachable and enjoyable.

Aesthetic design is not just about making things look good; it is about crafting an experience that resonates with users, fostering a deeper connection with the software. As technology continues to evolve, the role of aesthetics in programming will become increasingly important, shaping the future of user interaction in profound ways.

Chapter 13: Mindfulness in Coding

Focus and Attention

In the realm of programming, focus and attention are not mere cognitive faculties; they are the bedrock upon which effective coding practices are built. The programmer's mind, akin to a finely tuned instrument, requires a disciplined approach to harness these mental capabilities to their fullest potential. To understand the intricate relationship between focus and programming, we must delve into the cognitive processes that underpin these skills.

Focus, in the context of programming, refers to the ability to concentrate on a specific task or problem without succumbing to distractions. This mental state is characterized by sustained attention, wherein the programmer is fully immersed in the task at hand. The neural mechanisms underlying focus involve the prefrontal cortex, which is responsible for executive functions such as decision-making, problem-solving, and maintaining attention on relevant tasks.

Attention, on the other hand, is a broader cognitive process that encompasses the ability to selectively concentrate on specific stimuli while ignoring others. It involves both the capacity to sustain focus over prolonged periods and the ability to shift attention as needed. This duality of attention is crucial in programming, as it allows for the seamless transition between different aspects of a project, such as debugging, coding, and testing.

The interplay between focus and attention is critical in programming environments, where distractions are ubiquitous. The modern programmer often faces an array of potential disruptions, ranging from digital notifications to environmental noise. To mitigate these, programmers must cultivate strategies to enhance their focus and attention. One such strategy is the practice of mindfulness, which involves maintaining a non-judgmental awareness of the present moment. Mindfulness has been shown to improve attention regulation, thereby enhancing the programmer's ability to maintain focus on coding tasks.

Moreover, the role of attention in problem-solving cannot be overstated. When faced with complex coding challenges, programmers must employ selective attention to identify relevant information and filter out extraneous data. This process, known as attentional control, is essential for efficient problem-solving and is facilitated by an organized approach to coding. By structuring code logically and employing modular design principles, programmers can reduce cognitive load and improve attentional focus.

The impact of focus and attention on programming performance is further evidenced by the phenomenon of flow. Flow is a state of optimal experience characterized by complete absorption in an activity, where the individual experiences a sense of control and intrinsic motivation. In programming, achieving a flow state can lead to heightened productivity and creativity, as the programmer is able to engage deeply with the coding process. The conditions necessary for flow include clear goals, immediate feedback, and a balance between challenge and skill level.

Ultimately, the cultivation of focus and attention is not merely a cognitive pursuit but a practical necessity for programmers seeking to excel in their craft. By understanding the underlying cognitive processes and implementing strategies to enhance these faculties, programmers can optimize their mental resources and achieve greater success in their coding endeavors. The programmer's mind, when disciplined in focus and attention, becomes a powerful tool capable of navigating the complexities of the digital landscape with precision and clarity.

Reducing Distractions

In the intricate landscape of a programmer's mind, distractions emerge as formidable adversaries. These interruptions, whether external or internal, can significantly impair cognitive functions, leading to decreased productivity and diminished quality of work. Recognizing the pervasive nature of distractions is the first step toward mitigating their impact.

External distractions, such as ambient noise, unsolicited notifications, and interruptions from colleagues, are ubiquitous in modern work environments. These disturbances can derail focus and fragment attention, imposing cognitive switching costs that burden the working memory. The implementation of environmental controls, such as noise-canceling headphones or designated quiet hours, can serve as effective barriers against such disruptions.

Moreover, the digital workspace is rife with potential distractions. The very tools designed to aid productivity, such as email clients, messaging apps, and social media platforms, often become sources of interruption. Strategies to mitigate these include the use of software that blocks distracting sites, scheduling specific times for checking emails, and employing "deep work" sessions where notifications are silenced.

Internal distractions, although less visible, are equally insidious. These are often rooted in cognitive processes such as wandering thoughts, stress, and fatigue. The human brain has a natural tendency to seek novelty, which can lead to a drift of focus away from the task at hand. Mindfulness practices, such as meditation and focused breathing, have been shown to enhance concentration and reduce the propensity for the mind to wander.

Additionally, the concept of task management plays a crucial role. The brain is more efficient when it can focus on one task at a time, rather than juggling multiple tasks simultaneously. The adoption of methodologies like the Pomodoro Technique, which involves working in focused bursts with scheduled breaks, can optimize mental resources and sustain attention over extended periods.

A crucial factor in managing distractions is understanding the role of fatigue. Mental fatigue can exacerbate the impact of distractions, reducing the brain's capacity to filter irrelevant stimuli. Ensuring adequate rest, nutrition, and physical activity can bolster cognitive resilience and enhance the ability to maintain focus.

The importance of a structured routine cannot be overstated. Establishing a predictable schedule can help the brain anticipate periods of work and rest, optimizing its alertness and readiness to engage with tasks. This predictability aids in minimizing cognitive load, as the brain requires less effort to transition between activities.

Furthermore, the personalization of strategies to reduce distractions is vital. Each programmer's cognitive architecture is unique, and what works for one individual may not be effective for another. Experimentation with different techniques and adjustments to the work environment can help identify the most effective personalized strategies.

In the dynamic and demanding realm of programming, the ability to manage and reduce distractions is a pivotal skill. By adopting a multifaceted approach that addresses both external and internal sources of distraction, programmers can enhance their cognitive performance, leading to improved productivity and a more efficient problem-solving process.

Mindful Workflows

In the realm of programming, the ability to maintain focus and clarity amidst the cacophony of daily tasks is paramount. The concept of mindful workflows emerges as a pivotal strategy in achieving such composure, allowing programmers to navigate complex environments with precision and efficiency. This approach is not merely about managing tasks but involves cultivating an awareness that aligns mental processes with the technical challenges at hand.

Mindful workflows begin with the identification and prioritization of tasks, a process that necessitates a deep understanding of the project's goals and the individual steps required to achieve them. By breaking down larger objectives into manageable components, programmers can address each segment with full attention, minimizing cognitive overload. This segmentation facilitates a structured approach to problem-solving, where each task is treated as a distinct entity within the broader context of the project.

Central to this methodology is the practice of single-tasking, which stands in stark contrast to the often glorified concept of multitasking. Single-tasking emphasizes the importance of dedicating one's full attention to a single task at a time, thereby reducing the potential for errors and enhancing the quality of the output. This practice is supported by cognitive science, which suggests that the human brain is better equipped to process information sequentially rather than simultaneously.

Another critical component of mindful workflows is the incorporation of regular breaks and intervals of rest. The Pomodoro Technique, for instance, advocates for a cycle of focused work followed by short breaks, optimizing mental sharpness and preventing burnout. Such techniques are grounded in research that highlights the cognitive benefits of rest periods, which allow for the consolidation of information and the rejuvenation of mental resources.

The environment in which programming takes place also plays a significant role in fostering mindfulness. A well-organized and clutter-free workspace can significantly enhance focus, reducing distractions and promoting a sense of calm. Furthermore, the use of tools that aid in task management, such as digital kanban boards or time-tracking applications, can support the maintenance of mindful workflows by providing visual cues and reminders of progress.

Mindful workflows are further bolstered by the practice of reflection, where programmers periodically assess their progress and methodologies. This reflective practice encourages continuous improvement, enabling individuals to identify areas for development and to adapt their strategies accordingly. Through reflection, programmers can cultivate a deeper understanding of their work habits and the impact these habits have on their productivity and well-being.

In essence, mindful workflows represent a holistic approach to programming, where technical proficiency is intertwined with mental clarity and focus. By emphasizing the importance of attention, organization, and reflection, programmers can not only enhance their productivity but also foster a greater sense of satisfaction and engagement with their work. As the demands of the programming profession continue to evolve, the adoption of mindful workflows offers a sustainable path forward, ensuring that both the mind and the code remain in harmony.

Work-Life Balance

In the realm of software development, the intersection of personal and professional time often blurs, posing significant challenges to maintaining a healthy work-life balance. For programmers, whose work involves intricate problem-solving and continuous learning, the risk of burnout becomes a pervasive concern. This subchapter delves into the dynamics of achieving equilibrium between work and personal life, emphasizing strategies that can foster well-being and productivity.

Central to the discourse on work-life balance is the concept of boundary management. Programmers frequently operate in environments that demand high cognitive engagement and prolonged periods of concentration. The advent of remote work exacerbates this, as the physical separation between home and office diminishes. Establishing clear boundaries is crucial; this includes setting definitive start and end times for work, creating a dedicated workspace, and communicating these limits to colleagues and family alike.

Equally important is the notion of time management. Efficient time allocation can significantly alleviate the pressure of impending deadlines. Techniques such as time blocking—allocating specific periods for focused work, breaks, and personal activities—can enhance productivity and ensure that personal time is safeguarded. The Pomodoro Technique, which involves working in short, focused bursts followed by brief breaks, is a particularly popular method among programmers for maintaining concentration without succumbing to fatigue.

Furthermore, the integration of leisure and relaxation into daily routines is paramount. Regular physical activity, whether through structured exercise or casual movement, serves as an effective counterbalance to the sedentary nature of programming work. Engaging in hobbies and activities that diverge from screen time can provide mental respite and stimulate creativity, indirectly benefiting professional output.

The psychological aspect of work-life balance cannot be overstated. Mindfulness and stress management techniques, such as meditation and deep-breathing exercises, are instrumental in maintaining mental clarity and emotional resilience. These practices can help programmers navigate the high-pressure environments typical of software development, reducing the risk of burnout and promoting long-term career sustainability.

Moreover, fostering a supportive work culture that prioritizes employee well-being is essential. Organizations can play a pivotal role by encouraging flexible work arrangements, promoting regular breaks, and recognizing the importance of personal time. Peer support networks and mentorship programs can also provide valuable platforms for sharing experiences and strategies related to work-life balance.

Technological tools offer additional support in managing work-life dynamics. Applications designed for task management, communication, and collaboration can streamline workflows, reducing the cognitive load on programmers. However, it is imperative to use these tools judiciously, ensuring they do not encroach upon personal time or contribute to digital fatigue.

Ultimately, the pursuit of work-life balance is an ongoing process, requiring continuous reflection and adaptation. By implementing deliberate strategies and fostering an environment conducive to well-being, programmers can achieve a harmonious integration of their professional and personal lives, enhancing both their productivity and quality of life. This balance not only benefits individual programmers but also contributes to the overall health and success of the organizations they serve.

Mindful Communication

In the realm of software development, effective communication stands as a cornerstone of project success, yet it is often underestimated or overlooked. Mindful communication, a concept deeply rooted in awareness and intentionality, offers a framework for enhancing interpersonal interactions within programming teams. This subchapter delves into the principles and practices of mindful communication, aiming to equip programmers with the tools necessary for fostering a collaborative and understanding work environment.

The essence of mindful communication lies in the deliberate and conscious engagement with others, characterized by an acute awareness of one's thoughts, emotions, and responses. This awareness extends to the acknowledgment of the communicative context, encompassing both verbal and non-verbal cues. For programmers, who often navigate complex technical discussions, the ability to remain present and attentive to the nuances of communication is paramount.

One fundamental aspect of mindful communication is active listening. This involves more than merely hearing words; it requires a deep engagement with the speaker's message, reflecting an understanding that goes beyond the surface. In practice, active listening entails minimizing distractions, maintaining eye contact, and providing feedback that demonstrates comprehension and empathy. A programmer who masters active listening can decode the underlying concerns and intentions within a team discussion, leading to more effective problem-solving and innovation.

Equally important is the articulation of thoughts in a clear and considerate manner. Clarity in communication ensures that ideas are conveyed without ambiguity, reducing the potential for misunderstandings that can derail projects.

Mindful communicators are adept at structuring their messages logically, tailoring their language to the audience, and using analogies or examples to bridge gaps in understanding. This skill is particularly vital in cross-functional teams, where technical jargon must be translated into accessible language for non-technical stakeholders.

Mindful communication also encompasses the regulation of emotional responses. The high-pressure environment of software development can sometimes lead to stress and frustration, which, if unchecked, can manifest in unproductive interactions. By cultivating emotional awareness, programmers can recognize their emotional triggers and adopt strategies to manage them constructively. Techniques such as pausing before responding, deep breathing, and reframing negative thoughts contribute to maintaining a calm and composed demeanor, even in challenging situations.

Moreover, the practice of empathy plays a critical role in mindful communication. Empathy involves the ability to understand and share the feelings of others, fostering a sense of connection and mutual respect. In a programming context, empathic communication can bridge the gap between diverse team members, each bringing unique perspectives and experiences. By valuing and acknowledging these differences, a team can harness its collective strengths, driving creativity and cohesion.

Mindful communication is not an innate skill but one that requires continuous cultivation and reflection. Regular feedback sessions, mindfulness exercises, and communication workshops can serve as valuable tools for programmers seeking to enhance their communicative competence. As teams strive to innovate and adapt in an ever-evolving technological landscape, the integration of mindful communication practices can serve as a catalyst for collaboration, understanding, and success. Through intentional and thoughtful engagement, programmers can transform their interactions into powerful tools for building stronger, more resilient teams.

Chapter 14: The Global Impact of Code

Technology and Society

The interrelation between technology and society is a complex and evolving phenomenon, deeply rooted in the very fabric of human progress. As we delve into the world of programming and its impact, it is imperative to acknowledge how technological advancements have shaped societal norms, values, and structures. The intricate dance between innovation and social change has been a defining characteristic of modern civilization, with programming at its core as a catalyst for transformation.

In the realm of technology, programming stands as a pivotal force that drives the digital age. From the inception of simple algorithms to the development of sophisticated artificial intelligence systems, programming has redefined how society interacts with technology. The rise of programming languages and tools has empowered individuals and industries to create solutions that address complex societal challenges, from healthcare and education to communication and entertainment.

The influence of programming on society is evident in the way it has democratized access to information and resources. The internet, powered by intricate networks of code, has become a global repository of knowledge, enabling individuals from diverse backgrounds to access information previously restricted to a select few. This democratization has spurred a cultural shift towards inclusivity and equality, challenging traditional power dynamics and fostering an environment where innovation is accessible to all.

Moreover, programming has played a critical role in shaping economic landscapes. The proliferation of software-driven industries has transformed labor markets, creating new opportunities while rendering certain skills obsolete. As automation and machine learning continue to advance, society faces the dual challenge of harnessing these technologies for economic growth while addressing the displacement of workers. This necessitates a reevaluation of educational systems to equip future generations with the skills needed to thrive in a technology-driven world.

The societal implications of programming extend beyond economics and education, influencing ethical considerations and privacy concerns. The capacity to collect, analyze, and utilize vast amounts of data has raised questions about individual privacy and the ethical use of information. As programmers develop systems that increasingly permeate daily life, the responsibility to uphold ethical standards and protect user privacy becomes paramount. This underscores the need for a robust framework that balances innovation with ethical considerations, ensuring technology serves the greater good.

Furthermore, programming has facilitated the emergence of virtual communities and platforms that transcend geographical boundaries. Social media, online forums, and collaborative platforms have redefined interpersonal communication, allowing individuals to connect and collaborate in unprecedented ways. These digital communities have become breeding grounds for cultural exchange and collective action, fostering a sense of global interconnectedness.

As we navigate the complexities of a technology-driven society, it is essential to recognize the symbiotic relationship between programming and societal evolution. The dynamic interplay between technological innovation and social change continues to shape the human experience, offering both opportunities and challenges. By understanding this relationship, we can better anticipate the future trajectories of technology and society, ensuring that the benefits of programming are harnessed to enhance the quality of life for all.

Global Collaboration

In the rapidly evolving field of software development, the ability to collaborate effectively across global boundaries has become essential. As technology continues to transcend geographical limitations, programmers are now more interconnected than ever before. This interconnectedness introduces both opportunities and challenges that necessitate a refined approach to collaborative software development.

Global collaboration in programming allows for a diverse range of perspectives and expertise. When individuals from different cultural and educational backgrounds come together, they bring unique problem-solving approaches and innovative ideas to the table. This diversity can lead to more creative solutions and a broader understanding of user needs worldwide. However, harnessing this diversity requires a well-structured approach to communication and coordination.

Communication remains a cornerstone of successful global collaboration. With team members potentially spread across multiple time zones, asynchronous communication tools become invaluable. Platforms such as GitHub, Slack, and Jira facilitate seamless interaction, allowing team members to contribute without being hindered by temporal constraints.

These tools not only support code sharing and review but also maintain a continuous dialogue among contributors, fostering a sense of community and shared purpose.

Moreover, the adoption of standardized coding practices and documentation is crucial in a globally distributed team. Adhering to a common set of coding standards ensures that all team members can understand and contribute to the codebase without misinterpretation. Comprehensive documentation further aids in bridging gaps, providing clear guidelines on system architecture, code functionality, and project goals. This uniformity helps mitigate potential misunderstandings and ensures that everyone is aligned toward the same objectives.

Time zone differences, while a challenge, can be leveraged to maintain a continuous development cycle. With team members working in staggered shifts, projects can progress around the clock, reducing downtime and accelerating product development. This requires meticulous planning and a robust handover process to ensure that each shift transition is smooth and productive.

Cultural sensitivity and awareness are also indispensable in fostering a collaborative environment. Understanding cultural nuances and communication styles can prevent misinterpretations and build stronger interpersonal relationships. Encouraging an inclusive atmosphere where all voices are heard and respected enhances team cohesion and morale.

Technological advancements have facilitated global collaboration by providing tools that support distributed version control, automated testing, and continuous integration. These tools enable teams to manage code changes efficiently, ensuring that integration issues are identified and resolved swiftly. Automated workflows further streamline the development process, allowing teams to focus on innovation rather than mundane tasks.

Security is another critical aspect of global collaboration. Protecting intellectual property and sensitive data requires robust security protocols and practices. Implementing secure authentication methods, regular security audits, and adherence to data protection regulations are essential in safeguarding collaborative efforts.

Ultimately, the success of global collaboration in programming hinges on the ability to align diverse talents toward a common goal. By embracing diversity, fostering effective communication, and leveraging technological tools, programmers can unlock the full potential of global collaboration. This not only enhances individual projects but also contributes to the broader advancement of the software development industry, paving the way for more innovative and inclusive technological solutions.

Digital Divide

The rapid evolution of technology has permeated almost every aspect of modern life, leading to significant advancements in programming and software development. However, it has also exacerbated disparities between those who have access to digital technologies and those who do not, a phenomenon known as the digital divide. This divide is not merely a matter of having or lacking technology; it encompasses a broader spectrum of issues, including access to information, the ability to effectively use digital tools, and the socio-economic factors that influence these capabilities.

The digital divide is multifaceted, influencing and reflecting disparities in education, economic status, and geographic location. Individuals in urban areas often enjoy high-speed internet and access to the latest digital tools, whereas those in rural or economically disadvantaged regions may struggle with limited connectivity and outdated equipment. The implications of this divide extend beyond mere access to technology; they affect the ability of individuals to participate in the digital economy, access educational resources, and engage with the broader global community.

From a programmer's perspective, understanding the digital divide is essential for developing inclusive software solutions. Programmers must consider the accessibility of their applications, ensuring they are usable on a variety of devices and platforms, including those with lower processing power or limited internet connectivity. This requires a keen awareness of the constraints faced by users in different environments and a commitment to designing software that is both resource-efficient and user-friendly.

Moreover, the digital divide has implications for the programming workforce itself. Individuals from underrepresented communities may face barriers to entering the field due to a lack of access to foundational resources, such as reliable internet, programming tools, and educational opportunities. Addressing these barriers is critical for fostering a diverse and innovative programming community. Initiatives aimed at providing free or low-cost access to coding education and resources can help bridge this gap, enabling a broader range of individuals to contribute to and benefit from the digital economy.

The role of policy makers and educators in bridging the digital divide cannot be overstated. Governments and educational institutions must work collaboratively to ensure equitable access to digital infrastructure and resources. This includes investing in broadband infrastructure in underserved areas, supporting digital literacy programs, and incorporating computer science education into school curricula from an early age. By fostering an environment that values and supports digital literacy, society can help mitigate the effects of the digital divide and empower individuals to become active participants in the digital world.

In the context of a programmer's mind, the digital divide highlights the importance of empathy and social consciousness in software development. Programmers are not merely creators of technology; they are architects of digital experiences that can either bridge or widen societal gaps. By prioritizing inclusivity and accessibility in their work, programmers can contribute to a more equitable digital landscape. This involves not only technical considerations but also a deep understanding of the social and cultural factors that influence technology use.

In summary, the digital divide presents both challenges and opportunities for programmers. By acknowledging and addressing these disparities, programmers can play a pivotal role in shaping a digital future that is inclusive and accessible to all. This requires a commitment to continuous learning, collaboration, and innovation, ensuring that the benefits of technology are shared equitably across society. As technology continues to evolve, so too must our approaches to bridging the digital divide, ensuring that no one is left behind in the digital age.

Open Source Movements

The evolution of open source movements represents a transformative shift in the software industry, influencing not only how software is developed and distributed but also how it is perceived and utilized by programmers and organizations globally. At its core, the open source paradigm challenges traditional proprietary software models by advocating for transparency, collaboration, and community-driven development.

The origins of open source can be traced back to the collaborative ethos of early computing communities, where sharing code and ideas was a norm. This spirit of collaboration was formalized with the inception of the Free Software Foundation in 1985 by Richard Stallman, who introduced the concept of "free software"—defined by the freedoms to use, study, modify, and distribute software. These principles laid the groundwork for the open source movement, which gained momentum in the 1990s with the emergence of projects such as the Linux operating system.

Linux, perhaps the most emblematic open source project, demonstrated the viability of large-scale, collaborative software development. Thousands of developers worldwide contributed to its codebase, resulting in a robust, flexible, and secure operating system. The success of Linux catalyzed the growth of other open source projects, leading to the establishment of platforms like GitHub, which facilitate collaboration by providing tools for version control and project management.

The adoption of open source software by enterprises marked a significant turning point. Organizations began to recognize the strategic advantages of open source, including reduced costs, increased security through transparency, and the ability to customize software to specific needs. Major corporations, such as IBM and Google, invested heavily in open source projects, contributing to their development and integrating them into their business strategies. This corporate embrace further legitimized open source as a cornerstone of modern software development.

Open source movements have also influenced the cultural and ethical dimensions of programming. They promote a culture of inclusivity and knowledge sharing, where the barriers to entry are lowered, allowing a diverse range of contributors to participate. This democratization of software development fosters innovation and accelerates technological progress, as a multitude of perspectives and skills converge to solve complex problems.

Despite its many benefits, the open source model is not without challenges. The reliance on voluntary contributions can lead to issues of sustainability and resource allocation. Moreover, the decentralized nature of open source projects can complicate governance and decision-making processes. Efforts to address these challenges have led to the development of formal governance structures and funding models to ensure the longevity and health of open source ecosystems.

In the contemporary landscape, open source movements continue to evolve, adapting to new technological advancements and societal needs. The proliferation of artificial intelligence, machine learning, and cloud computing has opened new avenues for open source innovation, as developers collaborate to build tools and frameworks that drive the next wave of technological transformation.

Ultimately, open source movements embody the ideals of collaboration and shared knowledge, challenging conventional notions of ownership and control in software development. As these movements continue to grow and adapt, they remain a testament to the power of collective human ingenuity in shaping the future of technology.

Cultural Influences

The programming landscape is intricately shaped by a multitude of cultural influences. These influences permeate the fabric of software development, affecting the ways in which programmers conceptualize, design, and implement solutions. Understanding these cultural aspects provides a deeper insight into the nuances of programming practices across different global contexts.

One of the most significant impacts of culture on programming is the variation in problem-solving approaches. Cultures that emphasize individualism may foster environments where programmers are encouraged to innovate independently, potentially leading to groundbreaking solutions. Conversely, collectivist cultures might prioritize collaborative efforts, resulting in a more cohesive development process. This dichotomy influences not only the outcomes of projects but also the methodologies adopted by programming teams.

Language is another critical cultural factor that affects programming. The syntax and semantics of programming languages often reflect the linguistic structures inherent to their creators' native tongues. For example, the preference for certain naming conventions and code structuring in languages can be traced back to cultural norms and linguistic patterns. This can present challenges in global teams, where programmers must navigate these differences to maintain code clarity and consistency.

Moreover, cultural attitudes towards risk and failure can significantly shape programming practices. In cultures where risk-taking is encouraged, programmers might be more inclined to experiment with cutting-edge technologies and unconventional methods. This can lead to rapid innovation but also increases the potential for errors and setbacks. On the other hand, cultures that view failure more negatively may promote a more cautious approach, prioritizing stability and reliability over rapid advancement.

The cultural context also influences the tools and technologies that gain popularity within a region. Socio-economic factors, educational systems, and governmental policies can all play a role in determining which programming languages and frameworks are taught and used extensively. This results in a diverse array of technological ecosystems, each with its own strengths and limitations.

Another aspect of cultural influence is the perception of time and deadlines. Cultures that operate on a monochronic time orientation, where tasks are approached sequentially and deadlines are rigid, may develop software with a strong emphasis on punctuality and process adherence. In contrast, polychronic cultures, which view time more flexibly, might prioritize adaptability and creative problem-solving, potentially leading to more dynamic and responsive software solutions.

Additionally, the hierarchical structures prevalent in different cultures can affect decision-making processes within programming teams. In high-power distance cultures, decisions may be centralized, with senior developers and managers having significant influence over the development process. This can lead to efficient decision-making but may stifle creativity from less senior team members. Conversely, low-power distance cultures may encourage a more egalitarian approach, fostering an environment where ideas from all levels are considered, enhancing innovation and team cohesion.

Understanding these cultural influences is crucial for programmers working in increasingly globalized teams. It allows for more effective communication, collaboration, and integration of diverse perspectives, ultimately enriching the programming process and outcomes. By appreciating the cultural dimensions of programming, developers can navigate the complexities of international projects more adeptly, ensuring that their contributions are both relevant and impactful on a global scale.

Chapter 15: The Journey of a Programmer

Career Paths

In the labyrinthine world of programming, aspiring coders often find themselves at a crossroads of potential career trajectories. This chapter explores the myriad paths available within the vast realm of software development and engineering, each offering distinct challenges and opportunities. The diversity of roles in this field is a testament to its dynamic nature, driven by rapid technological advancements and the ever-evolving demands of the digital landscape.

Software development, a cornerstone of programming careers, encompasses a broad spectrum of roles ranging from front-end development, which focuses on the user interface and experience, to back-end development, dealing with the server side of applications. Full-stack developers, who possess expertise in both areas, enjoy a holistic understanding of the entire application process, making them highly versatile and sought after in the job market.

Beyond traditional development roles, the rise of data science has opened new avenues for programmers with a penchant for statistics and analytics. Data scientists and analysts leverage programming skills to interpret complex datasets, deriving insights that drive strategic business decisions. This field requires a robust understanding of programming languages such as Python and R, combined with knowledge of machine learning algorithms and data visualization techniques.

The increasing reliance on cloud computing has also paved the way for careers in DevOps and cloud engineering. These roles emphasize the integration and automation of software processes, ensuring seamless deployment and operation of applications across cloud platforms. Mastery of tools like Docker, Kubernetes, and cloud services such as AWS or Azure is essential for success in this domain, highlighting the importance of staying abreast of technological trends.

Cybersecurity, another critical area, demands programmers who are adept at identifying and mitigating threats to digital infrastructure. As cyber threats become more sophisticated, the need for skilled professionals in this field continues to grow. Careers in cybersecurity often involve roles such as ethical hacking, penetration testing, and security analysis, where programmers employ their skills to safeguard data and systems.

Moreover, the realm of artificial intelligence and machine learning presents exciting opportunities for programmers interested in developing intelligent systems. This field requires a deep understanding of algorithms, neural networks, and frameworks like TensorFlow or PyTorch, and is characterized by its potential to revolutionize industries through automation and innovative solutions.

The game development industry also offers a unique career path for programmers with a passion for creativity and storytelling. Game developers and software engineers in this sector work on designing, coding, and testing interactive games, often collaborating closely with artists and designers to bring immersive experiences to life.

Each of these career paths requires a specific set of skills and knowledge, yet they all share a common foundation in programming principles. Whether one chooses to specialize in a particular domain or explore multiple areas, continuous learning and adaptability are crucial in navigating the ever-changing landscape of the programming world. By understanding the diverse possibilities within this field, aspiring programmers can better chart their career paths, aligning their interests and skills with the demands of the industry.

From Novice to Expert

Understanding the evolution from novice to expert within the domain of programming requires an examination of cognitive processes, problem-solving skills, and the accumulation of domain-specific knowledge. The transformation is not merely a function of time spent programming but is deeply rooted in the ability to internalize complex concepts and apply them in novel situations.

At the novice level, programmers are typically focused on syntax and the basic structure of programming languages. Their cognitive load is heavily taxed by the need to remember rules and syntax, often leading to a trial-and-error approach to coding. Novices tend to view problems in isolation, lacking the broader context that comes with experience. Their solutions are often inefficient and lack robustness, primarily because their understanding is limited to superficial characteristics rather than underlying principles.

As programmers progress, they develop a deeper understanding of programming paradigms and begin to recognize patterns across different problems. This stage is characterized by the transition from rule-based reasoning to more strategic problem-solving. Programmers begin to appreciate the importance of algorithms and data structures, understanding their role in optimizing performance and resource management. The cognitive load decreases as familiarity with language constructs increases, allowing for more focus on problem-solving rather than syntax.

With further experience, programmers start to internalize best practices and design principles, such as modularity, abstraction, and code reuse. They become adept at anticipating potential pitfalls and debugging becomes a more intuitive process. The expert programmer possesses a mental repository of patterns and solutions, enabling them to quickly identify the most efficient path to a solution.

Experts are distinguished by their ability to apply their knowledge flexibly across a wide range of problems. They possess a deep understanding of the intricacies of multiple programming languages and can choose the most appropriate tools and techniques for a given task. Their solutions are not only effective but also elegant, reflecting a sophisticated understanding of both the problem domain and the tools at their disposal.

The culmination of this journey is the ability to innovate. Expert programmers contribute to the evolution of programming languages and paradigms, pushing the boundaries of what is possible. They are not confined by existing frameworks but are capable of creating new ones, driven by a profound understanding of the underlying principles of computing.

In essence, the transition from novice to expert in programming is marked by a shift from a focus on individual components to a holistic understanding of systems. It involves the development of a mindset that embraces complexity and seeks simplicity within it. This transformation is a testament to the adaptability of the human mind and its capacity to navigate the intricate landscape of programming, turning abstract concepts into concrete applications that drive technological advancement. Through continuous learning and adaptation, programmers evolve from novices who follow instructions to experts who create them, embodying the dynamic nature of the field itself.

Mentorship and Growth

Mentorship in programming serves as a pivotal mechanism for fostering both individual and collective growth within the software development ecosystem. This process is characterized by a symbiotic relationship between seasoned developers and novices, where knowledge transfer is facilitated through structured guidance, collaboration, and feedback. Such an environment not only accelerates skill acquisition but also cultivates a culture of continuous learning and adaptability essential for navigating the ever-evolving technological landscape.

The role of a mentor extends beyond mere technical instruction. It encompasses the nurturing of critical thinking, problem-solving capabilities, and the inculcation of best practices that align with industry standards. Through mentorship, novices gain insights into code optimization, design patterns, and efficient debugging techniques, thereby enhancing their proficiency and confidence in tackling complex projects.

Moreover, mentorship contributes to the development of soft skills, which are indispensable in a collaborative work setting. Effective communication, teamwork, and leadership abilities are honed as mentees engage in pair programming, code reviews, and project management discussions. These interactions foster a sense of community and belonging, reducing the isolation often experienced in solitary coding environments.

From the mentor's perspective, the relationship is equally enriching. It provides an opportunity to refine their own understanding through teaching, as explaining concepts to others necessitates a thorough comprehension of the subject matter. Additionally, mentoring encourages mentors to stay abreast of the latest technological advancements and trends, ensuring they remain relevant in a rapidly changing field.

The growth facilitated by mentorship is not linear but rather exponential. As mentees progress, they often transition into mentoring roles themselves, perpetuating a cycle of knowledge dissemination and professional development. This cyclical process contributes to the resilience and dynamism of the programming community, as each generation builds upon the foundations laid by their predecessors.

Incorporating mentorship programs within organizations yields tangible benefits. It reduces the learning curve for new hires, thereby increasing productivity and reducing the time to market for software products. Furthermore, it enhances employee satisfaction and retention, as individuals feel valued and supported in their professional journeys.

To maximize the impact of mentorship, it is crucial to establish clear objectives and expectations. Regular feedback sessions, goal setting, and progress tracking are essential components of a successful mentorship arrangement. These mechanisms ensure that both parties remain aligned and committed to the developmental objectives.

Organizations should also strive to create an inclusive and diverse mentoring environment. Diversity in mentorship encourages the exchange of varied perspectives and ideas, fostering innovation and creativity. By embracing diversity, the programming community can address existing biases and create solutions that cater to a broader audience.

Ultimately, mentorship is an indispensable element in the cultivation of a robust programming culture. It bridges the gap between theoretical knowledge and practical application, equipping individuals with the tools necessary to excel in their careers. Through mentorship, programmers are empowered to contribute meaningfully to their teams and the broader technological landscape, driving progress and innovation.

Lifelong Learning

In the rapidly evolving landscape of technology, the necessity for programmers to continually update and expand their knowledge base has become paramount. This subchapter delves into the concept of lifelong learning within the context of programming, exploring its significance, methodologies, and the impact on both individual careers and the broader technological ecosystem.

The programming industry is characterized by its dynamic nature, with new languages, frameworks, and tools emerging at an unprecedented pace. Programmers are often compelled to adapt quickly to these changes to maintain their relevance and effectiveness. The ability to learn continuously is no longer a luxury but a critical skill that can determine a programmer's success in the field.

The importance of lifelong learning in programming is underscored by the rapid obsolescence of technologies. A language or tool that is popular today may become outdated tomorrow. Thus, programmers must be adept at not only learning new technologies but also discerning which ones have long-term viability. This requires a keen understanding of industry trends and the foresight to anticipate the future needs of the market.

Methodologies for lifelong learning in programming are varied, reflecting the diverse learning styles and preferences of individuals. Self-directed learning, facilitated by online resources such as tutorials, webinars, and coding platforms, allows programmers to tailor their learning experiences to their specific needs and pace. Formal education, through courses and certifications, provides structured learning paths and validation of skills. Collaborative learning, enabled by communities such as open-source projects and coding forums, offers opportunities for knowledge exchange and problem-solving with peers.

The role of mentorship and peer interaction in lifelong learning cannot be overstated. Engaging with more experienced programmers can provide valuable insights and guidance, helping novice programmers navigate the complexities of the field. Conversely, mentoring others reinforces one's own knowledge and fosters a collaborative spirit within the programming community.

The impact of lifelong learning extends beyond individual career advancement. It contributes to the collective growth of the technological ecosystem. As programmers continuously enhance their skills and knowledge, they drive innovation, improve software quality, and contribute to the development of more efficient and effective technological solutions. This, in turn, propels the industry forward, creating a cycle of continuous improvement and innovation.

Moreover, lifelong learning promotes adaptability and resilience, qualities that are essential in an industry prone to rapid changes and uncertainties. Programmers who embrace lifelong learning are better equipped to handle shifts in technology and market demands, enabling them to pivot and thrive in diverse environments.

In conclusion, the pursuit of lifelong learning is a fundamental aspect of a programmer's professional journey. It is a proactive approach that not only enhances individual capabilities but also enriches the programming community as a whole. By continuously seeking knowledge and embracing new challenges, programmers can sustain their competitive edge, contribute to technological advancements, and shape the future of the industry. The commitment to lifelong learning is, therefore, not just a professional obligation but a strategic imperative in the ever-evolving world of programming.

Personal Narratives

In the realm of computer programming, personal narratives serve as a powerful medium to explore the intricate relationship between the human mind and the digital world. These narratives are not mere stories but reflections of the cognitive processes that drive creativity, problem-solving, and innovation within programming.

The act of programming is often perceived as a logic-driven endeavor, grounded in algorithms and data structures. Yet, beneath this structured exterior lies a deeply personal experience, shaped by individual thought patterns, emotional responses, and unique perspectives. Each programmer, through their narrative, reveals a distinctive approach to crafting code, one that is as varied and complex as the human mind itself.

Consider the cognitive processes involved in debugging a complex piece of software. The programmer must navigate a maze of potential errors, utilizing both analytical skills and intuition. This process is akin to unraveling a mystery, where each clue is a line of code, and each breakthrough is a moment of personal triumph. The narrative here is one of persistence and resilience, highlighting the emotional rollercoaster that accompanies the resolution of a stubborn bug.

Moreover, programming narratives often reflect the broader context of the programmer's life. The environment, cultural background, and personal experiences inform the way programmers perceive problems and devise solutions. A developer from a resource-constrained setting might prioritize efficiency and optimization, while one with access to extensive resources may focus on innovation and feature-rich applications. These narratives underscore the diversity of thought and approach that enriches the programming community.

The collaborative nature of modern programming further accentuates the importance of personal narratives. Open-source projects, for instance, are a tapestry woven from the contributions of countless individuals, each bringing their narrative to the collective whole. Through code comments, commit messages, and documentation, programmers share their thought processes, challenges, and insights. These narratives foster a sense of community and continuity, allowing others to build upon past work and advance the field.

Personal narratives in programming also serve as a bridge between technical expertise and human understanding. They offer a glimpse into the motivations and aspirations that drive individuals to pursue programming, whether it be the joy of creating, the satisfaction of solving complex problems, or the desire to make a meaningful impact. Such narratives humanize the field, making it accessible and relatable to those outside the technical sphere.

In documenting these narratives, programmers contribute to the collective knowledge base, providing invaluable resources for both novices and seasoned practitioners. These stories are repositories of lessons learned, offering guidance and inspiration to those navigating the challenges of programming. They remind us that behind every line of code is a human story, rich with personal insights and experiences.

Ultimately, personal narratives in programming illuminate the dynamic interplay between the human mind and technology. They celebrate the diversity of thought and the shared journey of discovery and innovation. Through these narratives, we gain a deeper appreciation of the programmer's mind, recognizing it as a wellspring of creativity and ingenuity in the digital age.